"Simple enough to follow for a mom with two crazy toddlers. The chaos can stay at the playground because I now have a system and plan that doesn't require chaos."

—Samantha Lane

"Very informative, and gives me the confidence to pursue this as a business as everything is step-by-step and well-explained. As a novice investor, this goes a long way in building the confidence required to go ahead."

—Dan Herard

"Easy to follow, codified common sense. The senior tips were fantastic and showed real value. I was looking for a system to use as a framework for my vision and I got it!"

—Sarah Ivey

"All Canadian, extremely well-organized. Learned so much — wish I had known this a long time ago. Has given me structured information so I can get started immediately. One of the most informative pieces of information has been the suggestion to specialize geographically; I had been thinking 'all over the place.'"

—Sandra Tong

"If you are even considering real estate as part of your portfolio, you would be skipping a major part of your due diligence if you did not review the REIN system."

—Claudio Gambetti

"Wish I had joined REIN three years ago when I read the book."

—Peter Rollings

"Outstanding! Your life is a reflection of the expectation of your peer group. Make REIN your peer group and your support system and you will soon see yourself as a professional real estate investor with your own portfolio sharing your own success story and helping others. REIN offers at least 100 times more than what you would normally get for the price."

—Marek Soltys

81 FINANCIAL AND TAX TIPS FOR THE CANADIAN REAL ESTATE INVESTOR

Also by Don R. Campbell

Real Estate Investing in Canada: Creating Wealth with the ACRE System,
2nd Edition

Also by Don R. Campbell with Barry McGuire, Peter Kinch, and
Russell Westcott

97 Tips for Canadian Real Estate Investors
51 Success Stories from Canadian Real Estate Investors

81 FINANCIAL AND TAX TIPS FOR THE CANADIAN REAL ESTATE INVESTOR

EXPERT MONEY-SAVING ADVICE ON ACCOUNTING AND TAX PLANNING

DON R. CAMPBELL

PRESIDENT OF THE REAL ESTATE INVESTMENT NETWORK

NAVAZ MURJI, CGA | GEORGE E. DUBE, MAcc, CA

John Wiley & Sons Canada, Ltd.

Library and Archives Canada Cataloguing in Publication

Campbell, Don R.
  81 financial and tax tips for the Canadian real estate investor : expert money-saving advice on accounting and tax planning / Don R. Campbell, Navaz Murji and George E. Dube

Includes index.
ISBN 978-0-470-73683-8

  1. Real estate investment–Canada.   2. Real estate investment–Taxation– Canada.   I. Murji, Navaz.   II. Dube, George E., 1971- .   III. Title.   IV. Title: Eighty-one financial and tax tips for the Canadian real estate investor.

HD316.C316 2009   332.63'240971   C2009-905173-7

The material in this publication is provided for information purposes only. Laws, regulations, and procedures are constantly changing, and the examples given are intended to be general guidelines only. This book is sold with the understanding that neither the author nor the publisher is engaged in rendering professional advice. It is strongly recommended that legal, accounting, tax, financial, insurance, and other advice or assistance be obtained before acting on any information contained in this book. If such advice or other assistance is required, the personal services of a competent professional should be sought.

Production Credits
Cover design: Adrian So
Typesetting: Thomson Digital
Printer: Friesens

Editorial Credits
Editor: Don Loney
Project Coordinator: Pauline Ricablanca

John Wiley & Sons Canada, Ltd.
6045 Freemont Blvd.
Mississauga, Ontario
L5R 4J3

Printed in the United States of America

10 9 8 7

TABLE OF CONTENTS

100% of the Author Royalties from this book (as well as Don Campbell's other bestsellers, *Real Estate Investing in Canada 2.0*, *97 Tips for Canadian Real Estate Investors 2.0*, *51 Success Stories from Canadian Real Estate Investors*, *Secrets of the Real Estate Cycle*, and *Real Estate Joint Ventures*) are donated directly to Habitat for Humanity to assist those in our society who need a hand up. To date, more than $830,000 has been raised through these books and the generous assistance of the members of the Real Estate Investment Network for this worthy cause. For more details, please visit the real estate discussion forums at www.myREINspace.com.

Introduction

It's Not How Much You Make — It's How Much You Keep — That Matters

This book is unlike any Canadian real estate book ever published. It targets two key areas for investors — financial management and tax — and is ideal for those who want to ensure their real estate investments are profitable by implementing simple tips and strategies to increase profits and lower taxes.

Losing sight of the financial and tax implications of real estate investing is easy to do because people get caught up in the excitement of the buying and selling of property. However, you neglect these fundamentals at your own financial and emotional peril.

What you will learn: How to make more money with your real estate investments, and keep more of that profit in your bank account.

What you will NOT learn: How to take stupid risks, hide your money off shore or trick the Canada Revenue Agency (CRA). The strategies and concepts taught here are not about tax avoidance; they are about profit and tax management. We live in one of the best countries in the world, and paying tax is a cost of living here. The key is to only pay the tax that you need to, not any extra.

This Knowledge is YOUR Responsibility — Not Your Accountant's

Ignorance is never a defense. Over the last 18 years, I have witnessed countless investors blindly abdicate financial responsibility to their accountants and lawyers. We all need these professionals in our lives, since without them, our businesses would be a mess. However, they still work *for* you and *for* your business and that is an important distinction you never want to forget.

What investors must understand is that, at the end of the day, the buck (and all responsibility for the decisions) stops with them. The professionals they have on their team have many, many clients that they are juggling and doing their best to advise on an ongoing basis. These individuals provide investors with options based on their knowledge. However, at the end of the day, it is the investor's job to know why he or she is signing a document (and what that document is) or making a claim to the CRA. And that is why this book is so important for Canadian investors. It is designed to provide you with clear knowledge and strategies you can start using today to get the best return on your investment dollar.

Investors who become complacent about financial and tax aspects of their business will 100% compromise their success. Put this book to good use.

NO THEORY, JUST REAL LIFE

81 Financial and Tax Tips for the Canadian Real Estate Investor has been written for you by veteran accountants who are also experienced property investors. This is a critical fact. Tax and accounting theories are important to know, but often the theories don't work well in real life. In addition, tax court decisions change the rules of the investment game on an almost monthly basis and that is why listening to an accountant who also owns investment real estate is so important. Informed and experienced accounting professionals keep on top of these ongoing changes to take care of their own money, and then transfer that knowledge to their clients' portfolios.

By combining their many years of accounting and real estate investing, the authors of this book ensure that the tips and strategies you are about to discover really do work in the real world and will make a positive difference to your bottom line and increase your financial management IQ (FM IQ).

As we discovered in *Real Estate Investing in Canada 2.0*, every investor is the president and CEO of his or her real estate investment portfolio, no matter what the size of that portfolio might be. That book, along with others in the series, including *97 Tips for Canadian Real Estate Investors 2.0*, taught readers the importance of building a team of professionals that includes real estate agents, mortgage brokers, property inspectors, lawyers and accountants who can give you sound business advice based on real-world experience.

This book will not replace the advice you receive from these professionals. Moreover, it is clearly not "accounting advice." Instead, it is written to arm you with specific action steps and money-saving tips you can begin using right away. This book is meant for people who like a no-nonsense approach to ideas about how they can make (and save!) money while investing in Canadian real estate.

Veterans and beginners are urged to read this book with a highlighter and pen handy and to be prepared to have some of your current thinking turned upside down. While it's true that some of the tips may be considered controversial and even counter-intuitive, that's what helps make them so effective. Whether saving you dollars or making you more dollars, it really is all about how much you keep at the end of the day.

So, read this book, implement the tips along with your accountant, and watch your bottom line grow.

Don R. Campbell
President of the Real Estate Investment Network
Author of the bestseller *Real Estate Investing in Canada 2.0*
www.realestateinvestingincanada.com

PART 1

GET HELP!
QUALITY INFORMATION
IS THE FASTEST WAY TO
INCREASE YOUR FM IQ!

TIP #1: THE TRUTH ABOUT DEATH AND TAXES.

You can't avoid death. You can't avoid taxes. Now get on with running a profitable business.

It's human nature that when we make money, we want to keep it. For some that involves trying to shelter money from the tax collector. This can be done through intelligent and lawful tax strategies, or through not-so-lawful means. The wise investor knows exactly where to park their business bus: focus on a business that makes money. Paying tax comes with the territory, and the more you pay, the more you have made.

Parts 5 and 6 of this book will guide the reader through the Canadian tax system. In the meantime, it's good to remind ourselves that taxes are a fact of life in Canada, where three levels of government collect taxes. The federal government collects taxes via income tax based on your income, personal and corporate sales taxes (HST, GST, alcohol, fuel, cigarettes, etc.), corporate capital taxes (based on your assets, not income), and various fees such as EI, CPP, licensing, royalties and more.

Provincial governments collect income taxes that generally blend in your federal income taxes, sales taxes (except Alberta), corporate capital taxes (based on assets or liabilities) and various fees such as royalties and licensing. Alberta has some components of tax that are independent of the federal government, and Quebec collects its own taxes.

Municipal governments generally collect property taxes, business taxes, builders' fees and licensing fees. There is very little connection between municipal government and your income taxes paid to the other two levels of government.

🕐 KEY INSIGHT

Governments do not have money. All of their money comes from some form of taxation. Individuals and businesses essentially act as government "trustees" in that they pay the costs associated with collecting taxes and then remit the money to the government. A good trustee knows the rules!

🅢 SOPHISTICATED INVESTOR TIP

You are in business to make money

The majority of taxes are pro-rated based on the amount of income generated. Sophisticated real estate investors recognize there are two ways to make money: you can trade time for dollars through employment or running a business, or you can learn to make your money work for you and reap the benefit of passive income. *Real Estate Investing in Canada 2.0* shows readers how they can transition from paid employment to full-time investing, or incorporate a part-time approach that's respectful of the individual investor's tolerance for risk.

Regardless of where you are on that spectrum, always remember that you are in business to make money. As an investor, this means you must assess the risk and take investment action when warranted. Investment decisions should be viewed over a long period of time (10-to-20-years minimum) and should never be focused on schemes that aim to avoid taxes. The real purpose of investment income is to get rich, slowly. This approach takes all of the "excitement" out of investing because it focuses on using tried-and-true investing approaches.

For a refresher on the fundamentals of a tried-and-true investing approach, review Appendix 1. The information gleaned from the Property Goldmine Score Card is essential to risk management in a sophisticated real estate investing system.

🅥 RED FLAG

When it comes to tax shelters, be aware that investment schemes marketed as "tax shelters" are not all created equal. Generally speaking, where a loss is projected at some point in the first four years of a real estate project's life, the project is a tax shelter for tax purposes. But look behind the curtain. If the investment is not ultimately expected to make money, why are you investing in it?

NOTES:_____
_____
_____
_____
_____
_____
_____

TIP #2: ASSEMBLE YOUR TEAM.

Every decision you make has implications for financial management.

Real Estate Investing in Canada identified relationships as an essential part of real estate investing, with real estate agents, bankers or brokers, lawyers, accountants, property managers, tradespeople and co-venturers or co-investors, all supplying key components of a sophisticated real estate investment business team. So, gather your team, but always remember two important points:

1. You are responsible for every decision made; and
2. Every decision impacts financial management as long as it has the potential to affect profitability and the cost of doing business.

 **KEY INSIGHT**

Empower your team. Once you develop your team and the relationships are starting to strengthen, get out of the way! You provide the direction and parameters, but let these key members do what they do best.

NOTES:_____

_____

_____

_____

_____

_____

_____

_____

_____

_____

_____

TIP #3: HIRE A QUALIFIED ACCOUNTANT

Close and convenient are two of the worst reasons to contact the accountant-next-door!

An accountant with expertise in real estate investment will save you money by providing advice on tax strategies and sound bookkeeping practices. To make sure you're adding the right accountant to your investment team, novice investors need to ask prospective accountants a few questions before they bring them on board. You must determine if the accountant owns or has owned real estate as an investment and has clients who are active investors.

With email, couriers, phone meetings, web meetings, faxes and virtual offices simplifying real-time connections regardless of geography, the location of your accountant's physical office is much less important than his or her experience and availability. Sophisticated investors work with accountants whose client portfolios include a considerable number of active real estate investors. You get people who know what they're doing when you hire people who are already doing it!

NOTES:_____

_____

_____

_____

_____

_____

_____

_____

_____

TIP #4: GET TO KNOW HOW THE PROCESS OF AN ACCOUNTING PRACTICE WORKS.

Data compilation and the ability to meet deadlines matter, but you also want someone who can help you use that information to plan your professional and personal future.

Accountants charge by the hour or the job, and are deadline driven. As a sophisticated real estate investor, it's your job to look behind the hourly rate and determine if you are getting value for service. To do that, you need to understand that a great deal of an accountant's practice revolves around the compilation of data they need in order to fill out forms for personal taxes, corporate taxes, HST, GST, and so on.

You will want an accountant who is organized and has systems in place that boost efficiency. Most investors who think they can prepare their own data likely don't have systems in place to ensure that they have all the data they need. As you work through this book, you will see why tax preparation is no place for memory games!

 **KEY INSIGHT**

Your accountant must also be able to meet deadlines, including peak-period work when many clients must meet similar deadlines. It's your job to help your accountant meet those deadlines.

WHY DOES IT COST SO MUCH?

If you have questions about your accountant's fees, talk to him about what you can do to lower them. Accountants generally buy time from their staff or themselves and sell it to clients. If information is difficult to gather, you will pay for the time it takes an accountant to pull it together. Provide your accountant with receipts, statements of income, etc., in an organized way and at one time. Be available should your accountant have questions.

Rush jobs are another problem for accountants — and mean a higher bill for clients. When staff rush through jobs to meet deadlines, mistakes are made. A careful accountant will find the errors during review, but they take time to fix!

 SOPHISTICATED INVESTOR TIP

Accountants begin their tax season in the summer prior to the next year's deadline. This is when they review problems, create new templates and generally tinker with compilation and reporting systems. Take a look at some of the systems accountants have in place to help their clients:

1. *The "one-box" system.* Every client gets "one box" so there's no time wasted looking for documents.
2. *One file per desk.* To make sure file data is not compromised, only one file is open at a time.
3. *Set priorities.* Staff know what is required of them when they start a job. First A. Then B. Then C.
4. *Start and finish.* Complete the file you started. This saves the client money because there's no time lost when staff have to familiarize themselves with the information — again!
5. *Procedures. Procedures.* Standard documentation procedures are used so the accountants know how the information was obtained.
6. *Paperless files.* This saves time filing and retrieving papers. (Make sure you have good electronic back-up systems.)
7. *Dual screens.* Dual computer screens reduce errors.

KEY INSIGHT

A well-organized client helps his or her accountant meet deadlines by bringing them well-organized information early.

NOTES:_____

_____

_____

_____

_____

_____

_____

_____

_____

_____

TIP #5: THERE ARE QUESTIONS YOU *SHOULD NOT ASK* YOUR ACCOUNTANT.

Time is money. So keep your questions relevant and your answers real.

When dealing with your accountant, remember that time is money! Avoid debating issues where the tax savings at stake will save you less than the cost of the discussion and don't ask your accountant's office to send you extra copies of documents you will get as part of your file. (You do not need an extra copy of your tax return, for example.)

Here are some other discussions you should avoid having with your accountant:

1. **Never ask your accountant how you can hide a transaction from the Canada Revenue Agency.**
   Do not ask your accountant hypothetical questions with an illegal implication. Accountants are required to report certain transactions without your knowledge. This includes transactions under laws governing money laundering.

🚩 RED FLAG

The biggest argument for not asking how to do illegal transactions is that you risk becoming a "former client." Your accountant wants to do his job, not play games.

💡 KEY INSIGHT

Novice investors often hear about "grey area shortcuts" early in their investment careers. Someone might suggest you sign a document that's not true, assuring you it's a harmless and even necessary strategy. Investors who swim with sharks risk their money and their reputations. Don't do it!

2. **Do not ask your accountant for specific investment advice.**
   American entrepreneur Warren Buffet is one of the few people who really understands long-term investing — and even he makes some mistakes. Do not expect your accountant to do your due diligence. Your accountant is there to help you with administration set-up, advice or tax

issues. He is not trained to be an investor and most times will hedge on answering such questions for fear of lawsuits.

3. **Avoid hypothetical questions.**

   Novice investors may think it is a good idea to ask their accountant about all of the possibilities that may come with a particular investment or investment strategy. It is far better to focus on what you actually intend to do, while adding a few variables rather than a long list.

4. **Expect informed advice, not training.**

   Your accountant's practice is backed by years of education, training, experience and a commitment to continuous learning. Accountants cannot teach their clients everything they know, although they can teach the basics.

5. **Don't expect your accountant to take kindly to questions about the "latest date" you can bring in your documents.**

   Accountancy firms run on deadlines and you should want to help them do their job well. The closer your documents come in to the deadline, the greater the chance of error or a late filing and penalties.

6. **Your accountant cannot guarantee you will not be audited.**

   The best way to avoid being audited is to report all your income and claim zero expenses. This leaves little for the CRA to challenge. Since expenses are reported in order to reduce income and save tax, this is not a reasonable business practice!

7. **Information about what your friends "get away with" is not helpful.**

   You may know a guy whose accountant lets him write-off a Sea-doo. Be realistic in what you ask your accountant. All that really means is that your friend has not been caught. Similarly, you cannot get too creative with your expenses (laundry, shoes, baby safety items) and expect your accountant to look the other way. This is not a game and your accountant understands how concerns about minor items can attract major attention.

8. **But the CRA staff gave you a different answer . . .**

   CRA staff can be helpful, but they do not necessarily have the information to answer technical questions. The agency is also not bound by "decisions" rendered over the phone.

NOTES:_____

_____

_____

_____

TIP #6: LEARN TO READ
FINANCIAL STATEMENTS.

Make it your business to follow the money trail . . .

Financial statements show precisely where money comes and goes in a business. They are meant to be read and understood by the people who are responsible for that money. There are four main components of financial statements:

1. **Balance sheets** show what a business owns and owes at a given point in time. These are your assets, liabilities and shareholders' equity.
2. **Income statements** show how much money a business made and spent over a period of time. Income statements tell you how much revenue the business made in a given year or portion of that year, and what costs were associated with making/losing that money.
3. **Cash flow statements** detail the exchange of money between a business and outside entities over a period of time. An income statement tells you if the business made a profit. A cash flow statement tells you if it generated the cash it needs to pay its expenses and purchase assets.
4. **Statements of shareholders'/partners' equity** show changes in the interests of the business's shareholders over time.

🕛 KEY INSIGHT

You are in business to make money. Financial statements allow you to measure performance. Don't just read them, understand them.

NOTES:_____

_____

_____

_____

_____

_____

_____

_____

_____

_____

TIP #7: CHOOSE AND USE A
RECORD-KEEPING SYSTEM.

The best way to know if you're making money is to keep track of it!

Real estate investment offers lots of different ways to make money. Among other things, you can upgrade properties for resale, buy-and-hold rental units for cash flow and long-term appreciation, or hook up with co-venturers who put your money to work in real estate, or help you buy more properties for a mutual long-term gain.

Part 3 of this book gets into the nitty-gritty of financial records. Before we go there, we need to look at the fundamentals behind decisions about why financial records are so important.

First and foremost, when deciding how to manage your records, you need to recognize how the kind of investment you choose can dictate how much time you have to manage those records. (If you are the general contractor on a renovation site, long hours may keep you from doing much more than making sure receipts are put in a safe place!) That said, a lack of time to participate in detailed financial management on a daily basis is *no excuse* for not knowing the financial status of your business.

KEEPING FINANCIAL RECORDS

When people talk about accounting systems, they really mean a reporting system. Tip #8 looks at how you choose a computer program for your system. Before we go there, let's look at how an accounting system creates three reports on a historical cost basis.

1. **Income Statement.** This one starts on a certain date (for example, January 1) and goes to the next year. It shows all revenue and expenses and provides a net income/loss figure.
2. **Balance Sheet.** This shows what you own and what you owe on a given date, potentially December 31. It lists all properties, often at historical cost; meaning what you paid and your balance of all loans/mortgages. It shows your net equity at cost.
3. **Cash Flow Statement:** This is not the same as an income statement. You start with your income statement and add back non-cash expenses such as depreciation or Capital Cost Allowance (CCA). Then you deduct

the principal portion of loan repayments or include additional loans you obtained. Most co-venturers will want this report as they understand it from a cash perspective. Their accountants will want the income statement as that is required to file your personal tax return.

If you're new to real estate investing, or you are updating your reporting system, ask yourself:

1. **Who will use these reports?**
   You will need financial reports for tax purposes, lenders and co-venturers. The tax department needs an income statement for sure, and a balance sheet if you operate under a corporation. Today, tax authorities are requesting balance sheets even where properties are personally owned.
2. **How often will reports be required?**
   Most users will expect annual reports, but co-venturers may request monthly data. Find out what they need to see. The cost of producing detailed reports on a monthly basis may be prohibitive, especially if those properties are part of a 15-to-20-year plan.
3. **What information do users need?**
   Your banker and co-venturers will want an annual balance sheet. They may also want the following:
   a. **Cash Flow Statement.** This statement shows your net income, subtracts non-cash payments (e.g., amortization) and any principal repayments you make on your mortgage or loans, and subtracts building additions while adding cash receipts such as refinancing or additional investor funds.
   b. **Current Value Balance Sheet.** The investors and bankers want to know if the current value of your properties is up or down. Take the balance sheets and add a column for the current value of each property.
   c. **Key Ratios.** One key ratio shows the return on investment (ROI), while others show various liquidity and profitability ratios. The key ratio on investment takes the current value, including rental profits, less the original investment (or investment value at a particular time) to provide the accrued profit. This figure is then divided by the original investment (or investment value at a particular time), less any repayments.
   d. **Cash Forecast.** Shows how the properties are expected to perform in the next few years.

Cash Flow Statement (Income and Expense Spreadsheet)

Description	Total	
Rental Income	$—	
Late Fees Collected	$—	
Laundry and Other Income	$—	
(Less Vacancy)	$—	
Total Income		**$—**
Mortgage Interest	$—	
Bank Charges	$—	
Line of Credit Interest	$—	
Mortgage Interest Penalties	$—	
Legal Fees	$—	
Appraisal Fees	$—	
Accounting Fees	$—	
Bookkeeping Fees	$—	
Inspection Reports	$—	
Other Professional Fees	$—	
Insurance	$—	
Management Fees	$—	
Strata Fees	$—	
Advertising and Promotion	$—	
Meals and Entertainment	$—	
Repairs	$—	
Maintenance	$—	
Utilities—Rental Property	$—	
Property Taxes	$—	
Office at Home	$—	
Internet	$—	
Computer and Office Supplies	$—	
Travel	$—	
Motor Vehicle	$—	
Seminars	$—	
Miscellaneous	$—	
Total Operating Expenses		**$—**
Total Operating Income		**$—**

Description	Total	
Mortgage Principal Repayment	$—	
2nd Mortgage Repayment	$—	
Updates	$—	
Increase in Equity		$—
Net Cash Flow		$—

 KEY INSIGHT

It costs money to plan. But if you don't have a map to show where you're headed, you won't get there!

SOPHISTICATED INVESTOR ACTION STEP

Long before you have a Cash Flow Statement for each investment property in your portfolio, you will need to compile a Personal Cash Flow Summary and Net Worth Statement. Lenders will use these documents to determine whether you can afford the monthly payments of a mortgage, and experienced investors keep an up-to-date copy of this document in their Sophisticated Investment Binder. The binder, which helps lenders approve your deals, must also include a cover letter regarding your investment business, proof of income, a completed and signed mortgage application, a current credit bureau report, a revenue real estate asset statement, proof of down payment and prospective property information.

NOTES:_____
_____
_____
_____
_____
_____
_____
_____
_____

Tip #8: All record-keeping programs are not created equal.

Once you understand that your record-keeping system needs to generate financial reports for various users, you are ready to decide what kind of system will work best for you.

If you need to generate reports once a year, the simplest method is to take receipts and total them, by category, using an adding machine with a tape to keep track. Enter the numbers onto a spreadsheet and you have an Income Statement. This system sorts your receipts and lets you avoid reconciling bank and credit card statements, which takes times — and costs money!

Watch for duplicate receipts! They add to confusion as your book-keeper or accountant can easily forget and enter them twice. This means your tax return will be prepared based on incorrect documentation. Moreover, there is no benefit to submitting duplicate receipts, since you will have to pay for someone to sort the receipts and identify duplicates. Avoid the hassles by shredding duplicate receipts!

If you need more frequent reports, or need to generate reports on a number of properties, adopt a program that works for you, or one your bookkeeper is familiar with. QuickBooks is good if you/your bookkeeper is supervised by a qualified accountant. It allows you to make changes to transactions. Simply Accounting assumes you do not make errors. This means you may have to make "adjusting entries" to correct errors. Excel spread sheets also work well because they are easy to use and you do not need to understand double-entry bookkeeping systems.

 **KEY INSIGHT**

The authors of this book currently prefer QuickBooks over other programs. There are issues with QuickBooks, but as programs change every year (and are only as good as their users!), investors should investigate several programs and choose the one they best understand.

ⓢ Sophisticated Investor Tip

Do not re-invent the wheel!
by Connie Campbell

When I launched my bookkeeping business in 1992, a friend introduced me to the accounting software, Quicken (made by Intuit). Soon after loading

Sophisticated Investor Tip continues

the software onto my computer and entering our household expenses, I was hooked.

From there, I moved to QuickBooks, which was designed for book-keeping for companies. As my bookkeeping business grew, I converted my clients to this program and that led to a contract business with a local accounting firm. Forward-thinking accountants, they had bought into the QuickBooks phenomenon, but realized the software is only as good as the person entering the data!

At that time, Accpac and Simply Accounting (then called Bedford) were the mainstream programs and accountants were used to the fact that the only way to fix an erroneous error was to make an opposite entry. That kept most lay people confused. It also meant big fees for the accountants who inevitably had to make a lot of correcting entries to sort things out for their clients.

Before long, I was a QuickBooks expert and when our own real estate portfolio started growing, I recognized the need to set up an easy system that I could duplicate each time we purchased a unit. That led to a template for a very basic set of books. This same template eventually became the basis for my multi-family accounting.

This template, now widely adopted by members of the Real Estate Investment Network (REIN™), is based on a form developed by the Canada Revenue Agency. It enables you to record rental income and tracks what you spend. At the end of the year, you can print a report and use it, with very little adjustment, to file your taxes.

If you would like a free copy of this real estate-specific template, please send an email to info@reincanada.com. You will need the latest copy of QuickBooks before you put the template to work.

🚩 RED FLAG

Use the QuickBooks Closing Date Feature and you avoid corrupting tax data. If you enter transactions for 2012 but key in 2011 by mistake, your data for 2011 will be corrupted and your data for 2011 and 2012 will be wrong!

NOTES:_____

_____

_____

_____

_____

_____

TIP #9: KNOW WHEN TO TRANSITION FROM DIY TO BOOKKEEPER AND ACCOUNTANT.

Time is money. And since it costs money to make money, you need to figure out where your time is best spent. Finding property? Closing deals? Sorting receipts? Generating spreadsheets? Filing tax returns?

Real Estate Investing in Canada and *97 Tips for Canadian Real Estate Investors* walked readers through the advantages of professional property management. Regardless of whether you self-manage your portfolio or work with a property manager, this book assumes you — or someone you really trust — are tracking the daily expenses associated with each of your properties. It also assumes you have some professional accounting advice when it comes to filing your tax return.

If your financial records are behind and your "free" time is consumed with bookkeeping, you don't have the information you need to make business decisions. When your business operations are faltering because you're spending time sorting receipts instead of taking care of business, it's probably time to hire a bookkeeper to keep your financial records up-to-date and in order. Here's what you need to do:

1. Set up a system you and your bookkeeper can follow every month. You and the bookkeeper need to understand how and why specific items are recorded. Whether you choose an Excel spreadsheet or an accounting software program, the goal stays the same: You need a legible record of income and expenses.
2. Make sure the information the bookkeeper generates is the information your accountant needs. If it's not, you'll pay the accountant to get it right.
3. Ensure your bookkeeper and accountant can talk when necessary — and are available to answer your questions, too.
4. Your accountant can help your bookkeeper set up the cash forecast and current value/ROI data discussed in Tip #7. Generally speaking, you do not need an accountant to get you this information once your system is in place. If your accountant stays involved with this information, it will cost you. Think: Billable Hours! That said, you may well benefit from having your accountant help you monitor and interpret the information,

since their expertise can help you identify opportunities and issues. This can be done annually, quarterly or even monthly for more significant operations. Think: Value-Added!

KEY INSIGHT

Leverage is a powerful tool. If you want to use advanced investment strategies, like buying property with less than 20% down, you must be able to access current value/ROI information on properties you want to borrow against. If your property's value is going up, you can use that information to profit from your money—and the bank's. Again, numbers must be current!

SOPHISTICATED INVESTOR TIP

How to get value from your accountant
by Navaz Murji, CGA

Accountants provide two kinds of service: compliance and value-added. "Compliance" covers regular preparation and filing services such as tax returns, corporate financial statements, HST, GST, payroll, etc. "Value-added" service is where you ask questions for planning purposes prior to closing a deal. For example: How should I finance this property? I plan to close the deal this way—is that okay?

Sophisticated investors know they are responsible for the financial decisions they make. They also know that when you are getting professional advice, it's important to ask the right questions! Use the following suggestions to help you zero in on the right questions and make sure your accountant has the information he needs to give you sound advice.

1. When you think of a question, send an e-mail. This gives the accountant time to think about the question and formulate the appropriate response.
2. Make sure the question is real (not hypothetical) and has a tax or investment component.
3. If the deal closes tomorrow, your accountant's answer may not matter. This just frustrates them as their "advice" comes too late.

Sophisticated Investor Tip continues

4. If you do not get a response after a couple of days, phone. (A spam filter may have kept your message from getting through.)
5. Recognize your accountant's bias. Some are more positive towards long-term cash flow properties. Others may not like "flips," mutual funds, foreign exchange traders or day traders. Some may not like real estate at all! While the compliance side of accountants' training is similar, their life experience and investments are different — so find someone who fits with your long-term needs.

🔴 KEY INSIGHT

A good bookkeeper will save you money, since data entry work does not require a professional accountant's expertise. A professional accountant, however, will help you sort out bookkeeping problems and identify errors that could negatively impact business decisions and opportunities. Their jobs are both critical, but different.

NOTES:_____
_____
_____
_____
_____
_____
_____
_____
_____

TIP #10: KEEP IT SIMPLE. KEEP IT UP TO DATE!

A good system will help you minimize your year-end accounting fees.

You are in the real estate investment business to make money. That means you will pay taxes. It does not mean you should pay more than you have to!

The best way to get all the deductions you are entitled to receive is to accumulate proper documentation in a methodical fashion. Set up a proper system to:

1. Minimize your year-end accounting fees.
2. Collect all the income to which you are entitled.
3. Ensure that you do not overpay or pay multiple times for your expenses.
4. Prepare for that fateful day when the Canada Revenue Agency calls for an audit. (See Tips #59-#63.)

🅚 KEY INSIGHT

Understand the Ins and Outs of financial record-keeping. When money leaves your pocket, it goes to pay for something. Bookkeeping entries must follow the same pattern. A double-entry accounting system means that when you buy a new pipe for under a kitchen sink, the money has to "come" from somewhere and "go" somewhere. That's why you record it twice.

Owner's Account	Repairs & Maintenance
($42.87)	$ 42.87

NOTES:_____

_____

_____

_____

_____

_____

_____

_____

▲ INVESTOR-IN-ACTION: VALDEN PALM

Your systems must evolve with your business plan.

Valden Palm can zero in on the crux of his business with obvious ease: he buys and sells real estate to create long-term wealth. But "stuff" happens, even to seasoned investors, and when time and circumstances mean Valden has to get rid of a troublesome tenant or liquidate a property he'd bought for long-term-buy-and-hold, he relies on operational systems to keep his business on track.

Valden likes systems. On the tenant front, every business-related interaction with his tenants is systemized; meaning he can follow a template of action based on the situation at hand. If a tenant has a pet, Valden has a system to handle *all* the problems having a pet could create. That same philosophy kicks in if a tenant's cheque bounces. Valden simply calls up the appropriate system and follows it through. When a tenant gives notice, he reaches for his "move-out" system. Each of these systems is based on a simple, but tried-and-true, checklist developed from previous experiences or the experiences of others. (Valden is not fussy about who learns the lesson first!)

Valden uses systems to clear the lines of communications and set expectations for every business relationship, including his relationships with bookkeepers and accountants. He'll be the first to tell you that he depends on professional advice to lay out his choices. But when it comes to making the final decision, the buck stops with him.

Valden's success in real estate investment goes way beyond the sophisticated use of strategies involving RRSP funds or his innovative approach to finding quality properties to add to his portfolio. What really makes Valden's real estate business sustainable is the way he backs up a commitment to continuous improvement by never underestimating the relationship between his business plan and his tax strategies. Buy-and-sell decisions typically impact both, but not with equal results.

The tips covered in Part 1 delve into the basics of hiring the right members for your team and establishing lines of clear communication. The biggest take-home lesson from Valden's experience is that whenever you feel overwhelmed by the details, take a step back and find out what's *really* going on. In real estate, silence is *not* golden. Do talk to other investors about how they handle a problematic situation and seek professional accounting, tax or legal help where necessary. Then use that information to solve the issue. You might just get a new system out of the deal!

* * *

"In good times, when properties are turning over fast and everyone's excited about making a deal, it's very easy to take short cuts and forget the details. You tend to get lazy in the good times and that's just human nature. It's also an investor's biggest problem."

—Valden Palm

Some people know him as Mister Home Buyer and others call him Mister RRSP, but there's no confusion about why Valden Palm takes a template-like approach to his real estate business. First, people who use proven systems to help them make decisions end up with more time to be creative about how and where they find new real estate deals. Second, systems generate additional long-term wealth because they improve the way individual properties are managed. "Shortcuts," says Valden, "cost money."

Every once in a while, Valden answers his phone and hears the voice of his banker concerned about the size of Valden's account. "I see there's $300,000 just sitting in your bank account and I'm wondering if we could help." Valden Palm loves these calls. It's been a while since he's really had to take the advice of a banker, but he gets a kick out of knowing some of them worry he might not know how to put his money to work!

Valden's experience with systems comes from remembering what it's like to work without them. Investing in real estate since the late 1990s, Valden's first years were plagued by problems: problems with partners, problems with money, problems with properties. There was a time when the complications of real estate deals and relationships even compromised where his family lived.

That was then. Valden regrouped, struck out on his own and, from the outset, vowed to avoid as many mistakes as he could simply by learning from the mistakes others had already made. The first major step in that direction involved rejoining the Edmonton-branch of REIN (he had held a membership in B.C.). Some friends scoffed at his business plan, thinking "you bought rental property so you could be a kind of slum landlord." Valden had no desire to make money off the misfortune of others. He saw quality real estate investment as a way to help people by giving them a quality place to live. "I had to wrestle with some of my own fears, doubts and bad habits, too and I learned to see mistakes as lessons. What matters is that you learn the lesson — and move forward!"

His current portfolio focuses on residential properties and is a mix of town-houses, apartment condos, single-family homes and houses with suites, all in his home town, Edmonton. He uses his reputation as Mister Home Buyer to find and secure deals, often finding properties through what he calls the "secondary real estate market, a.k.a., the For Sale By Owner market." In recent years, Valden's also sold a number of his real estate holdings to compile cash to purchase some raw lands to re-zone for subdivision development. It's a natural step for ambitious senior investors trying to complement their portfolios by entering the subdivision market. "It gives them a new goal to shoot for," explains Valden. (Remember: Valden did this following systems that had already been proven. He made the jump only when he knew he had systems to back him up.)

Today's market is more complicated given the dramatic rise in Edmonton prices over 2007 and early 2008; especially since that market was followed by a dramatic economic decline. A complicated market isn't necessarily a bad thing, says Valden. "Honestly, you can buy in any market. You just buy differently."

You also manage differently. Since cash flow is important and there are fewer renters, well-managed, quality properties are king. Following proven market systems makes all of the difference. Again, that market demand is a good fit with Valden's systems, which already emphasize quality properties for quality tenants.

The RRSP Connection

A few years back, he took that same model and introduced a sister company, Mister RRSP. He got into that business after hearing how investors can use their fund and stock-based RRSP portfolios to invest in mortgages without having to cash out RRSP money (Tip #80). Drawn to the economic possibilities of tapping into the vast stores of RRSP funds held by Canadians, Valden created his own investment niche. Having studied, tested and mastered the RRSPs in real estate strategy, he now teaches other REIN members how to do it, too.

What never changed was his focus on making sure his business plans are always in step with his tax strategies. To make that happen, he relates to his accounting professionals as key players on his team. He's especially pleased when he takes them an idea, like selling Property "X" because he needs an influx of cash, and they get back to him with several scenarios about how that impacts his business and his tax position.

Rather than managing the situation after the fact, they are "happy to play the role of a dealer in a poker game where information manages the risks and the strategies. They don't want to be the one who plays the hand out. It's their job to give me the best cards they can and then I make the decision," says Valden. (Review Tip #5 for the reasons you should not expect your accountant to tell you what to do in a given situation. It's your money, so it's your decision.)

Because their knowledge of his business is so important, Valden also likes to work with the same accounting firm year-after-year. "Typically speaking, your business accountant is also the one working on your personal income tax. This means your accountant knows your entire financial landscape, and that can be really important when you ask for input about your choices. Personally, I want to do deal with someone who knows my situation and will help me work through several scenarios, because my final decision may have a long-term impact on my business and tax strategies."

Systems and good advice aside, Valden's also a big believer in recognizing where the buck stops with his real estate investment business. "The investor takes responsibility for the decisions," says Valden. "He gets the glory and he gets the pain."

* * *

ACTION STEPS

- ✓ Hindsight may be 20/20, but it's a bad way to run a business. Give your accountant the information he or she needs to give you choices about the decisions you could make.
- ✓ Recognize that business decisions have tax implications. Tax planning doesn't start the month before your statement is due. It's a year-round pursuit.
- ✓ Is your tax planner willing to talk about the really tough issues, like what might happen if your business partnership changes? He or she can help you structure a business to protect the profit-making assets.
- ✓ Who can you approach to learn more about investing RRSP money in real estate? Is this a niche your business should pursue?
- ✓ Who might you approach about investing RRSP funds in real estate? List three names to start.
- ✓ Don't get hung up on people who turn you down. Focus on action versus emotion.

PART 2

WHEN THERE IS MORE THAN ONE ANSWER . . . REAL ESTATE INVESTING IS COMPLICATED. AVOID COMMON PITFALLS.

TIP #11: COLLECT INFORMATION, NOT STORIES.

You are investing real money. Back up your decisions with real information.

You don't ask a medical secretary for medical advice, so don't count on your golfing buddy for real estate investment advice. When you hear stories about what others are doing, follow the sage advice of *Real Estate Investing in Canada* and *97 Tips for Real Estate Investors* — and *Look Behind The Curtain!* You want information built on sound principles to build a solid business. Bear these points in mind:

- Don't try and cheat the taxman.
- Develop a relationship with your accountant. Help him understand your business so you can seek relevant input.
- Avoid complicated schemes and offshore accounts when you are starting out.
- Seriously question advice gleaned from conversations in the pub.

🕐 KEY INSIGHT

Just because someone *thinks* they are a real estate investor doesn't make it true! Always seek advice from quality sources.

NOTES:_____

_____

_____

_____

_____

_____

_____

_____

_____

_____

TIP #12: FORGET FAIRNESS. IT'S ABOUT THE RULES.

When it comes to taxes, it's good to remember that while politicians and bureaucrats make the rules, it's your job to know how those rules apply to your business.

Politicians and bureaucrats make the rules. They do not necessarily understand (or even anticipate) how they will be interpreted by the Canada Revenue Agency staff and auditors. You do not need to like the rules. But you do need to understand how they affect you and your business, and you do need to follow them.

 **KEY INSIGHT**

If you're not an expert on the rules and changes, make sure your advisor is!

The CRA's Web site is www.cra.ca. This is where you will find the most up-to-date information about CRA rules, services and applications that promote compliance with Canada's *Income Tax Act* and regulations.

NOTES:_____
_____
_____
_____
_____
_____
_____
_____
_____

TIP #13: NEVER THINK YOU'RE SPECIAL!

Real estate investments are complicated transactions.

Sophisticated real estate investors know that tax rules are not personal. Never assume you can get away with something that is not permitted under the *Income Tax Act*. This act is law. It is also subject to an immense amount of interpretation. That does not mean the *Income Tax Act* is easy to circumvent. It does mean a different pair of CRA eyes may alter decisions and outcomes — even after you and your accountant have assumed a particular item has been dealt with. What is "allowed" this year may simply have been missed. If it's not in line with the general interpretation of the law, it will be retroactively disallowed when uncovered!

 **KEY INSIGHT**

You can challenge interpretations of the *Income Tax Act*, but there are time restrictions and you must live with the consequences. That means paying for disallowed deductions or tax credits, or risking exposure to an audit if those at the Canada Revenue Agency think your "creative accounting" means you may have paid less tax than you should have.

NOTES:_____
_____
_____
_____
_____
_____
_____
_____
_____
_____

TIP #14: REVIEW LEGAL AGREEMENTS FOR TAX CONSIDERATIONS.

Agreements with co-venturers may have unexpected tax implications. Ignorance is no excuse.

You can't un-spill milk and you can't retroactively undo the tax implications of a legal document. To make sure you and your co-venturers do not get an unwelcome surprise on your tax return, let your tax advisor review any legal documents related to co-venturers or other investment partnerships. Here are some issues that frequently arise:

- Does your co-venturer or partnership agreement represent co-ownership or a partnership? Each has different tax implications.
- Agreements with fixed disposition dates or criteria may strongly suggest a real estate investment will be taxed as "income" not "capital." (See Tip #53.)
- Unusual terminology or calculations related to the distribution of profits may attract the Canada Revenue Agency's attention.
- When corporations are involved, definitions regarding property ownership are important. Investors may provide a loan, invest into special or common shares in a company, have the company act as a "bare trustee" or have the company own a portion of the property on behalf of its shareholders while another portion of the property is owned by an independent individual or entity. Each option may provide or limit various tax advantages.
- Tax-withholding requirements related to non-resident owners may also come into play.

NOTES:_____
_____
_____
_____
_____
_____
_____

TIP #15: YOUR HOME IS YOUR CASTLE.

Your principal residence is the only real estate transaction that is tax free during your lifetime. Each family unit can only have one principal residence at a time.

The fact that we get a tax exemption for a principal residence seems straightforward enough. But this area has been identified by the Canada Revenue Agency as an area prone to abuse by taxpayers. Remember the golf buddy we talked about in Tip #11? The principal residence is a prime example of an area where bad information can cost you.

The big question seems to be: How long do I have to live in a home to qualify for a principal residence deduction? The answer is a lot more complicated than some investors believe.

Let's say you move into a new home. You take the old home and convert it into a rental property. At that point, you are deemed to have sold this property and you should get an appraisal. Chances are you have more equity in your old home and you will borrow money to buy the new property. This means you borrowed money to buy your new home, but the mortgage is on the first property. Now, you cannot deduct the interest from that first property. If you claim capital cost allowance (CCA) on this property (see Tip #57), you lose your principal residence exemption that may still be applicable in the future. This can happen accidentally if you do not clearly tell your accountant what you are doing, or if the move is overlooked in filing your tax return.

🔘 KEY INSIGHT

To avoid problems with the principal residence exemption, always keep your principal residence "clean" as far as CCA claims go. This means paying extra attention whenever "change of use" is involved.

What if you buy a fixer-upper, move in, fix it and sell it, or buy a teardown property, build a new property, move in, live there for awhile and then sell it? If you conduct a steady string of transactions, the CRA is more likely to take the position that you are in the business of buying and selling homes. The fact you live in them is simply convenience, so it will be taxed as regular income. That's right. You would lose your principal residence exemption and not qualify to get 50% of your income tax free by claiming a capital gain. In theory, this could happen on your first property!

HOW LONG IS ENOUGH?

So, how long do you have to live in a home to get your principal residence exemption? The jury's still out — and the answer depends on circumstances. Say, for example, you are a student and buy a pre-built one-bedroom condo that will be finished in two years. Upon completion, you move in. Three months later, you decide to get married and you do that six months later. You then sell your one-bedroom suite and move into a two-bedroom unit with your spouse. Here, you could probably argue that you are entitled to claim the principal residence exemption because your circumstances changed.

 RED FLAG

Always bring new accountants up to date on previous decisions! If your accountant doesn't know the history of your business, he may inadvertently claim capital cost allowance on a property without realizing he has just compromised your exemption on your principal residence.

NOTES:_____
_____
_____
_____
_____
_____
_____
_____
_____

TIP #16: ONCE YOU DECIDE WHO OWNS THE PROPERTY, YOU CAN'T CHANGE IT.

Decisions about whose name is on the title go way beyond tax.

Whose name should go on the title of your investment property? The question sounds innocent enough and is usually asked in reference to tax reduction. But that is only one consideration. From a business perspective, decisions about whose name goes on the title of investment property need to include future considerations like marital breakdown, which spouse is more likely to get sued (professionals!) and other legal issues a lawyer would have to address.

This tip zeroes in on the fundamentals of this decision to give novice investors real insight into what's behind the recommendations of their lawyers and accountants. For a more sophisticated strategy whereby you determine what *percentage* of a property each spouse might hold, see Tip #69.

A TAX PERSPECTIVE

In terms of tax, your objective with beneficial ownership is generally to split the income amongst the family unit so as to pay the lowest amount of tax. If the family unit means a husband, wife and young adult children, you need to project your other incomes, the property income during its lifetime, each of your prospective incomes when you sell the property, the expected selling price of the property and the expected tax rates. These are estimates, since no one can accurately predict the future. This projection will be based on reasonable expectations, since no one can foresee income changes based on lifestyle choices ranging from new babies to retirement dates and major capital spending plans.

SOPHISTICATED INVESTOR ACTION STEP

Consider the facts

Since you generally should not change the decision about who owns a property, you need to weigh several factors before the purchase closes. These include:

Sophisticated Investor Action Step continues

1. Annual income of the spouses.
    a. If the two spouses have similar incomes, a joint ownership may be appropriate because both are in similar brackets.
    b. If one spouse is working or one spouse is in a higher bracket, consider having the property in one spouse's name. If the property is profitable, you may want to put it in the name of the person with less income. If it's in a loss situation, it may be prudent to put it in the name of the person with the higher income initially, but later as the property becomes more profitable, this decision may be regretted.
2. Projected selling price of the property. In the year you sell the property, you want to report the income on the person in the lower bracket.
3. Where is the money coming from to acquire the property? You may not have as many choices where one spouse works and the other does not have a source of funds. That said, there are advanced tax planning strategies that can still be used, where done properly.

This is more complicated if the property is losing money, but is expected to have positive cash flow in a few years and be sold at a profit. Here, you must do an annual calculation with the expected tax savings each year by claiming the losses for the person with the higher income. It is not an easy calculation, but it will help you identify the preferred tax position!

🔵 KEY INSIGHT

Whose name goes on the title is the kind of question that needs to be settled long before you sign mortgage documents. Indeed, if you're close to signing, the mortgage company may deem a name change to equal a new application — so don't put off this decision until the end!

NOTES:_____

_____

_____

_____

_____

_____

_____

_____

TIP #17: INCORPORATING MY BUSINESS MAKES SENSE WHEN . . .

Just because you can incorporate, doesn't mean you should — and vice-versa. Weigh the advice of several professionals.

Four people walk into a bar: a lawyer, an insurance agent, a lender and an accountant. There is no punch line. When it comes to making the complex decision about incorporating your real estate investment business, those are four people whose professional opinions you should seek. And be forewarned: they will have different opinions and you will have to sort through that advice to make the decision that's right for you and your business.

Legally, incorporation is meant to protect you from frivolous lawsuits, unless the other entity goes after you personally as a director for being negligent. An insurance agent may tell you to forgo incorporation and buy the best liability insurance you can get (at least $1 million); topping that with an umbrella policy of $5 to $10 million. Talk to him about what happens when claims are made — and seek insight into lawsuits where insurance companies try to get out of paying claims.

On the lending side, expect your banker to ask for personal guarantees to borrow funds in a corporation. If that sounds unfair, ask yourself why a bank should lend you money if you are not prepared to demonstrate faith in the deal.

An accountant may approach the decision about incorporation from a more comprehensive position that includes a tax perspective. The bottom line is that every investor's situation is different, so there are no hard-and-fast rules about whether to incorporate or to own the properties in your own name. (Indeed, you should be wary of anyone who advises in a particular direction without a thorough knowledge of where your investment business is at and where you want it to go. What's "easiest" for some advisors may not be what's "best" for your business.) Because there are pros and cons to each scenario, it is critical that you approach your accountant for help in deciding what is the best in terms of taxes and liability.

Overall, income from passive sources, including rental income, is initially taxed at the highest rate; about 46% depending on the relevant province. This can be reduced to approximately 20% where dividends are paid to shareholders. Due to the tax-favoured treatment of dividends, these dividends may generate little or no personal income tax, but may be subjected to taxes at the rate of approximately 30%, depending on your income and province of residence. This potentially creates double taxation.

Active income is income from businesses such as retail, restaurants, professional practices, developers and rental income in a corporation with more than five full-time employees amongst associated companies. The first $500,000 of taxable income from these businesses is taxed at the low rate of corporate tax (about 16%, depending on your province, although some provincial limits increase at $400,000).

Beyond the general tax rates, a wide assortment of other tax issues will be revealed during your conversations about incorporation with your accountant. The most important thing to remember here is that *your* situation is unique and demands a unique approach.

 **KEY INSIGHT**

Decisions about incorporating your real estate investment business are complicated. Make sure you understand the pros and cons and why your advisors are making one recommendation versus another. When advice conflicts, dig deeper to discover what makes the most sense for your business. And remember: Doing nothing is a choice, too!

NOTES:_____

_____

_____

_____

_____

_____

_____

_____

_____

◆ INVESTOR-IN-ACTION: BRIAN PERSAUD

You have to be able to prove what you know.

What would it take to knock your real estate investment socks off? For Brian Persaud, it was hearing a trusted mentor tell him it was Brian's job to "Look behind the curtain" before he made any decisions. Brian thought he understood what due diligence meant before he heard that comment. But when that mentor told him to "Look behind the curtain," Brian realized just what was the true link between due diligence and personal responsibility. It was a lesson Brian liked. He already knew investors had to have a sense of the "big picture." Now he knew that the underlying details mattered more.

A full-time investor by the age of 25, Brian's savvy take on real estate investment soon earned him a regular spot on Rogers TV. With his own portfolio of residential real estate still in the growth phase, he is a testament to what happens when investors take the action necessary to get them to where they want to be.

This focus on action is important for two reasons. First, it takes action to find and buy properties and manage a portfolio. Second, real estate investing is about the creation of long-term wealth, but it's not meant to be a 40-plus-hours-a-week job. There will be weeks when it takes long hours to close a deal or solve a problem. But a good deal of the action an investor takes involves setting up the systems and relationships that reduce the stress involved with making sure that business runs well. That kind of action leaves more time to enjoy the rest of your life. Two notes of caution:

1. When it comes to success and the long hours associated with hard work, you can't have one without the other; and
2. Hard work is rarely exciting.

These two points really hit home on the record-keeping front. In this area, hard work often involves the near-constant replication of some pretty mundane tasks. You really do have to pick the right bank account (Tip #18), identify every deposit (Tip # 20), keep your records in meticulous order (Tip #23) and so on, and so on. *Do it, do it, do it.* As Brian's story shows, the results are *worth it, worth it, worth it.*

*　　*　　*

What you know is important. But what you don't know can really hurt you. Brian Persaud learned that the hard way. A university-student-turned-real-estate-investor, Brian figures his first investments included a lot of the same mistakes other novice investors make. With that experience safely tucked under his belt, he's not looking back.

A couple of years ago, Brian had a few major real estate deals go up in smoke. The experience burned. It also taught him he needed more control over the things that were actually in his control. In terms of due diligence, that meant he had to spend more time looking behind the curtain to find specific ways to reduce the risks he took with other people's money. He also needed to stop spending cash he didn't have.

To meet both goals, Brian committed to change the way he did business. First, he renewed his commitment to deals that worked for his money partners. That meant more focus on making sure everyone's needs were met, so expectations were managed in advance, which led to fewer surprises as deals progressed. Whereas he used to leave verbal discussions thinking (and sometimes acting) as if he had a formal deal in place, he now takes detailed meeting notes and follows them up with written confirmation about what he thinks went on. This opens the door for a final deal solidly based on details. "There are so many ways for a deal to fall apart. I think you really have to *will* a deal to happen. You have to work from the perspective that you really want that deal to be done and you have to be certain that the deal is solid."

He also moved his investment focus closer to home. His real estate experience to date had served him relatively well, but stressed by the fact that some of his properties were several provinces away, Brian saw some value in focusing on a particular geographic area. Following a system that promotes economic fundamentals, "I started researching the Toronto market and realized I didn't have to leave the province, or even the area, to find good properties," says Brian. Taking what he was learning about economic fundamentals, quality properties and quality tenants, Brian targeted the Toronto area and set out to find properties closer to home.

Since an investment business is about more than buying property, Brian also took a critical look at his record keeping. Determined to keep meticulous track of his cash flow, he went to his accountant for help. The accountant helped Brian set up financial records useful for business and tax planning. That includes a better system to track and file receipts so they are easily accessed when needed. Brian now puts each day's receipts in a special place in his office every day. He sorts through that pile once a week and places receipts into appropriate folders. He keeps the original receipts in case he's ever audited, but he and his accountant can work from the PDF files created by scanning the receipts. Brian concedes that scanning receipts takes time and it costs money when you pay someone else to do it. But that level of receipt organization makes Brian's accountant's job easier and faster, which also saves money. "My accountant takes care of the actual deductions and I provide whatever he needs to do that," says Brian, who figures he sees his accountant once a month.

A self-proclaimed high achiever who wants to grow his investment business as wisely as he can, Brian admits he takes a very disciplined approach to money. "Right now, I live off the cash flow of my real estate. That requires me to be very disciplined in terms of knowing exactly where my business is at. I do that because I have to," says Brian.

*   *   *

ACTION STEPS

✓ Commit to constant improvement: Set aside some time to think about your investment business. What's making money? What's not? What causes you stress? What comes easy? What do your answers to these questions tell you about what you need to change?

✓ Make change happen: Mediocrity is madness. Where can you go to learn how to strengthen your weaknesses? Who can you talk to? Where can you learn about "systems" you can adopt? What will you need to do to make sure you follow those systems?

✓ Write an action plan:
  – I will surround myself with people who are achieving what I want to achieve.
  – I will set up a lunch meeting with an investor who is willing to share her time and experience.
  – I will ask my accountant what I can do to make his job easier and thus save me money in the long run.
  – I will begin/end every day/week with a predetermined plan. This plan must include properly filing every piece of paper I have dealt with that day or week. (I will plan it into my daily agenda if that's what it takes to make it an operational business habit.)

- I will program my e-calendar to remind me about certain tasks that I need to take care of. (If I say I will look for properties Wednesday morning, I will block off the time to do that. If I say I want to review my mortgages three months before they're due, I will make time to do that. If I say I will file my receipts weekly and separate them into the appropriate folders (repairs/maintenance/entertainment/education) I will do that.

✓ Look for ways to build strong relationships with people who know more than you do:

Not everyone needs to meet their accountant every month. Do you need more extensive short-term help for long-term gain?

PART 3

FOR THE RECORD: YOUR NEW BUSINESS MANTRA: ORGANIZE AND DELEGATE. ORGANIZE AND DELEGATE.

TIP #18: PICK THE RIGHT BANK ACCOUNT.

Learn to avoid bank service charges.

A serious real estate investor needs a serious bank account. Right? Wrong. When you are in business to make money, you are also in business to avoid paying for things you don't need. And when it comes to banking, that includes fancy business cheques, important-looking bank statements — and good-for-nothing fees that add nothing to your bottom line!

Get personal. If you're the sole proprietor of your business, a personal account may be the best way to go. A personal account will generate the records you need and generally have lower fees.

Interest vs. No Interest. Bank options are never as straightforward as you might think. If you want to earn interest on your real estate business bank account, you may need to maintain a balance as high as $10,000. A no-interest account may need a much lower balance. When interest rates are low, a no-interest account may offer all you really need: free cheques, free stop payments, free travellers' cheques, free bank drafts.

Overdraft protection. This provides some protection when an outgoing cheque clears faster than an in-coming cheque. It can also help improve your credit rating, another bonus.

Be aware of systemic discrimination. Sophisticated investors can share horror stories about being denied preferential rates or even overdraft protection for reasons that really boil down to gender or youth. Yes, it is illegal to discriminate; yes, it still happens; and yes, if you do the work involved with selling your business to a lender, you will likely find someone who wants your business.

Look for a better deal. It pays to stay on top of what different banks are offering. You do want to build a good working relationship with a lender, but it's always good to know what the competition is offering . . . and then ask for it!

🕛 KEY INSIGHT

Sophisticated investors know it's good to have money in the bank. If you can carry a sizable bank balance (say, $25,000), you may be able to negotiate a bank deal whereby all fees are waived. Better yet, you have a great rainy day fund for contingencies (and a lot less stress!).

ⓢ SOPHISTICATED INVESTOR TIP

If at first you don't succeed . . .
by Connie Campbell

One of the things I learned when I was just starting out was a way to get the most out of my bank account.

My original bookkeeping business was named Connie and Co. Mobile Office Services. I had a cute business card with a logo that showed angel wings attached to a briefcase that was landing at full speed. I reckoned that briefcase should be flying *into* your business and not out of it. I soon learned to keep an eye on bank service fees, too, since it looked like money was flying out of my account and into the bank's pocket!

I was also very independent, as Don can attest. I wanted to re-invent the wheel back then, forging ahead and through. Lucky for me my instincts were great and I always landed on my feet (with my flying briefcase no less).

Instead of getting a joint bank account when we got married in the late 1980s, Don and I maintained separate ones. I firmly believed that I needed to retain my identity and credit rating. That made me a bit of a crusader, but I was fine with that.

At the time we were living on False Creek in Vancouver. I ventured up to Broadway and to the nearest bank. I had received my first loan from that same bank at the tender age of 18 when I purchased my first car with a loan co-signed by my father. I got a credit card at that time and presumed I was well on the way to my own identity.

No service fees
I opened a separate bank account for my flourishing bookkeeping business. As a sole proprietor, I was able to manage with a second personal account, which generally has lower fees. I also chose an account that would pay interest and waive all fees as long as you maintained a $10,000 balance. If you maintained a $2,000 balance, there was no interest, but fees were still waived. Looking ahead, I figured the $2,000 balance was a great way to maintain a rainy day fund. I didn't get the whopping 1.5% rate of interest I would have got with a minimum $10K balance, but I did not pay any fees and enjoyed numerous benefits including free cheques, free stop payments, free travellers' cheques and free bank drafts.

Sophisticated Investor Tip continues

After a couple of years in business, I read an article that said overdraft protection would help build my credit rating. I thought $5,000 overdraft protection was a done deal with this account, so re-visited the bank to get things set up.

Much to my surprise, I was rejected. An appointment with the bank manager revealed my approval was contingent on putting my husband's name on the application. I refused. The bank refused. I was devastated. The bank didn't care.

And then I fought back. By this time, Don and I were building a relationship with another banker. When I shared my tale and said I didn't want to be lumped in with Don's credit, this banker said he'd take care of it.

He immediately set up my own bank account with $5,000 in overdraft protection. But he also took it one step further. Because the other bank had gone in and "looked" at my credit without extending it, I now had a blemish on my credit report. This banker went so far as to make the opposite entry. He also filed a special note at the credit bureau saying credit had been extended, so the effect of the first inquiry was now offset by his extending the credit to me.

I closed all my accounts with the first bank and have been a loyal customer of the other bank ever since. I did eventually need that first bank's Merchant Services for a credit card, but this time the relationship was entirely on my terms. Today, we keep a $25,000 balance in return for having all fees waived. By operating as if the $25,000 is a zero balance, we have a healthy contingency for emergencies — and still avoid unnecessary bank fees.

⑤ SOPHISTICATED INVESTOR TIP

It pays to stay on top of what the banks are offering. With a little digging, you can find the account that matches your needs and you may be surprised at how little effort is required to get your fees down to nothing.

NOTES:_____

_____

_____

_____

_____

_____

TIP: #19: GET A SEPARATE BANK ACCOUNT FOR YOUR INVESTMENT BUSINESS.

It makes sense to have at least two bank accounts: one personal, one business.

Novice investors sometimes think they are saving themselves a lot of hassle if they stick to one bank account, since a single account means you only have one statement to review. Nothing could be further from the truth! While you may need to be able to transfer money into your business account from a personal account (an option you should secure when you open your business account), keeping a single bank account for your personal and business transactions invites confusion over whether certain transactions are for business or personal purposes.

Open a separate bank account for all of your real estate investment business transactions. This makes it easier for you to track money in and out, helping you make better business decisions and keeping the Canada Revenue Agency at bay.

Also make sure you can transfer money in and out with ease. If you need to meet an expense and there is a shortage of funds in the business account, you need to be able to transfer money into that account easily.

⑤ SOPHISTICATED INVESTOR TIP

NSF charges are for people who aren't paying attention! You do not want to be in that category.

NOTES:_____

_____

_____

_____

_____

_____

_____

_____

_____

Tip #20: Identify every deposit.

Use your bank statement as a reporting document!

All deposits to your bank account generally come from three sources:

1. A third-party loan.
2. Income.
3. Transfers from another bank account.

Bank statements do not necessarily identify the source of a deposit. If you don't identify the source of the deposit, the Canada Revenue Agency could argue that such a deposit is income. That leaves you exposed to taxes you shouldn't have to pay and you may have to prove it is *not* income you failed to report! The latter could result in "gross negligence" penalties potentially worth 50% (or more!) of the taxes payable.

This is not complicated — unless you have to identify the source of a deposit months or years later. What kind of deposits may be confused? If you're using a personal account, it could be anything from wages (or your spouse's wages), to inheritance and gift monies, and even tax refunds or loans. It could also be a reimbursement from a friend who owes you money for something entirely unrelated to your real estate investment business (like plane tickets to Mexico or his portion of a dinner out). If it is a loan and that's identified on your statement, it should at least jog your memory if you need to find supporting documentation.

⬤ RED FLAG

Novice investors may not realize how easy it is to lose track of deposits that are entirely unrelated to their investment businesses. Do not let yourself get caught!

⬤ SOPHISTICATED INVESTOR TIP

Make a copy of every cheque that is not a routine transaction for that bank account and keep all loan documents in your permanent file. Transfer these to your current file only after they are paid off.

🅢 SOPHISTICATED INVESTOR ACTION STEP

Put your bank statement to work

Your bank statements are a great place to start a good record-keeping system. With separate accounts for personal and investment purposes, you'll have less trouble tracking money in and out.

Get to know your bank statement

To make your bank statement the foundation of your record-keeping system, take a close look at what that statement does and does not tell you. Use the statement to provide an overall view of cash flow, but never neglect more detailed records.

Summary dates

Your statement is based on when that account was opened, and things can change between the date the statement is issued and the date you review the information. Much of your rental income, for example, will be due on the first day of every month. That may fall in the middle of your statement.

Details

The statement will show every transaction, from online banking activity to ATM withdrawals, Interac purchases, cheques, mortgage payments and loan credit.
  You need to:

- Review this information and check for accuracy.
- Make notes directly on the statement. This a good place to write notes about unexpected expenditures. You still need receipts, but this adds to the paper trail.
- Track cheques as the money moves out of your account. Deal promptly with any problems.
- Keep one account for **Personal Expenses** and a second for **Investment Expenses.** File the separate statements accordingly. If an Investment Expense goes through your personal account by accident, make sure you track the information so you don't lose a deduction.
- File the statements regularly.
- File by month or by year, depending on what works for your business.

NOTES:_____
_____

TIP #21: MANAGE YOUR BANK ACCOUNTS WITH CARE.

Bank statements are key components of a good record-keeping system.

A bank is where you keep your money. A **bank account** is a record of the flow of money. Investors should keep at least two accounts: one for personal expenses, the other for business. The Real Estate Investment Network recommends multiple accounts in a variety of cases. These include separate bank accounts for each co-venturer and a general investment account. Separate accounts for separate corporations are required by law if the company is active and many investors keep separate accounts for each property.

While separate bank accounts can be valuable, it can be confusing to manage multiple accounts. Here are some of the problems you need to guard against:

1. Make sure you write cheques *from* the right account.
2. Take care to deposit cheques *into* the right accounts.
3. When you need to pay one supplier from multiple bank accounts, you need to write multiple cheques.
4. Customers paying rent for multiple properties also need to write multiple cheques.
5. Each account needs to carry sufficient funds, especially if fund management is key to your bank fee.
6. Be mindful that banks may transfer funds to cover a shortfall, without your knowledge.
7. You will need to maintain a higher cash reserve as each account will need funds to operate.
8. You can expect higher accounting fees, since each account needs to be reconciled.

To guard against any of the problems noted above, an investor must commit to a regular and detailed review of his or her bank statements. Some investors take a quick look at their statements every day, while others set aside weekly and/or monthly sessions for more detailed evaluation. Regardless of your approach, this review is not something you can overlook. In addition to helping you track transactions related to each account, the bank statement can be your first line of defense against problems with negative cash flow. That can be an indication of problems with anything from property management to changes in the market fundamentals. Regardless of what's happening, early recognition of a problem paves the way for an early solution.

 **KEY INSIGHT**

Two accounts are better than one. Three and more are complicated. But the information generated by bank statements makes up a fundamental part of your record-keeping system, and a good paper trail will help with strategic business and tax planning.

RED FLAG

Any time you borrow funds, deposit them into the appropriate investment bank account. As long as the funds are used for qualifying investment-related expenses, the interest paid on the line of credit is deductible.

SOPHISTICATED INVESTOR TIP

Never mix any of your personal expenses with funds held in trust. Money and trust are sensitive to misunderstandings. Keep them clean.

NOTES:_____

_____

_____

_____

_____

_____

_____

_____

_____

TIP #22: SAVE THE STATEMENTS OF ADJUSTMENT AND TRUST LEDGER STATEMENTS FOR YOUR ACCOUNTANT.

Help your accountant help you!

The statement of adjustment and trust ledger statement provide a wealth of information to your accountant. The information is used to determine the correct total costs of the property and any required adjustments to the income for the period. It is also ideal for future reference, years from now, if the Canada Revenue Agency asks for evidence of the adjusted cost base of the property when the property is sold.

Avoid the pre-tax-deadline-scramble and forward these statements to your accountant as soon as you get them. This gives your accountant time to clarify entries, make his or her own notes and complete any work well in advance of the tax deadline rush. Remember Tip #4: The more you know about how the process of an accounting practice works with regard to data compilation and deadlines, the better you can control accounting costs and make sure your accountant has the information he or she needs to provide good advice.

🕐 KEY INSIGHT

Your accountant likely keeps this information in a permanent file, which will be a major asset if the CRA ever asks questions. Help your accountant keep the information current and send these statements to your accountant's office as soon as you receive them.

NOTES:_____

_____

_____

_____

_____

_____

_____

_____

_____

_____

Tip #23: Keep your records clean.

Messy financial records are unfinished business, and unfinished business will cost you money.

Unfinished business costs money. It costs in terms of bank fees, receipts you never claim, and deposits you have to pay tax on because you can't prove the money wasn't income. In the real estate world, good records are essential to help you, your bookkeeper and accountant compile the reports you need to make decisions.

You need to keep two sets of receipts: one set records expenses for the current year, the other for multiple years. These may include a loan that's taken out for three years, your mortgage documents, and purchase documents for properties and equipment. These should be filed into a permanent working paper file. You would transfer those into your current file when you sell property or equipment, or when you pay off a loan.

Because tax returns are filed annually, you need an annual filing system for tax purposes. For rental properties, have a file folder for each property. For expenses pertaining to more than one property that you own, have a folder for expenses that are common to all properties. Sort the receipts into categories such as fuel, advertising, bank charges, mortgage interest, and so on. At the end of each year, take these folders and summarize the total for each folder. This would be the amount that shows up in your tax returns. If you have lost a receipt, document that and leave it in the folder. Label these folders and store them in a box or envelope, then store them for future retrieval.

🔘 KEY INSIGHT

Follow the same format to label each file folder. Year. Property Name. Description of expenses.

For example: 2012. 123 Westcott Street. Repairs & Maintenance.

You can take these receipts to your accountant to prepare your tax return. Better yet, just give him or her the total! Then put all of the folders into a box or envelope and label it for the year.

Now go through your permanent files. Look for properties you have sold or mortgages you have refinanced and move them to the current year storages. If you sold a property in 2010, for example, you would file those papers with your current year's papers. This eliminates papers from your daily routine. Store this away and keep adding to the pile every year, be it boxes or envelopes. This way, if you need something from the year 2005, you can go to the envelope instead of sorting through 10 years of information.

KEY INSIGHT

Good records are easy to read, easy to understand and make it easy to provide a report to those who need to make good business decisions based on information in that report.

SOPHISTICATED INVESTOR TIP

We've said it before and we'll say it again: Experienced real estate investors deliberately seek ways to do the extra 10% it takes to make their businesses successful. They see value in keeping current and accessible records because they want to avoid the errors that come from working with inaccurate and hard-to-find business data and they apply that same approach to the compilation of their Sophisticated Investment Binders, which are discussed in detail in *Real Estate Investing in Canada*. By making three binders at once, sophisticated investors can give one to their lender, keep another handy for when unexpected deals come their way, and have a third as a master copy that's ready to be updated as new information becomes available.

NOTES:_____

_____

_____

_____

_____

_____

_____

_____

_____

TIP #24: RECORD LOAN PRINCIPAL AT THE TIME OF FINANCING.

Figure out how much you owe. That's a liability you need to understand — and track.

This tip highlights how good records can save you money. A surprisingly large number of real estate investors have no idea what they owe financial institutions for their mortgages. Accountants often see that mortgages are never reconciled with annual mortgage statements. Investors thus forgo a great opportunity to understand their true liability. And be forewarned: This is *not* a sophisticated strategy!

Investing greenhorns may wrongly assume that the proceeds advanced by an institution represent the total amount owed. This theory fails to consider the fees charged by the lender, plus any mortgage insurance fees. In reality, the total mortgage is often several thousand dollars more than the funds advanced by the lender.

How can this be? Well, you are only advanced a portion of the total loan, since the other fees need to be covered. Since money to pay those other fees was also loaned, it's not captured in the mortgage advance.

To see your total debt, make sure you review all of the legal documentation related to the loan. Verify that it matches your expectations of the mortgage as it was negotiated. With the details now confirmed, make a note of the total loan in your records. This allows you to track all of your debt, not just the funds advanced.

NOTES:_____

_____

_____

_____

_____

_____

_____

_____

_____

TIP #25: EMBRACE TECHNOLOGY THAT REDUCES RECORD-KEEPING ERRORS.

Look for ways to keep track of business transactions.

Some accounting software, including most of the most popular programs on the market, can generate three-part cheques. One part of the cheque is kept by you to attach, for example, to the bill you are paying. The second part, plus the cheque itself, are forwarded to the recipient for a detailed record of what you are paying. This helps with record-keeping and reduces transposition errors. These days, a lot of banks only provide one-part cheques unless you request otherwise — and you may not even get them back.

This is why you need access to a photocopy machine or scanner. Copy or scan:

- Invoices and attached copies of the cheques used to pay them.
- Letters sent to people who owe you money.
- Your credit card statement with notes about particular entries where you no longer have a receipt.

The ACRE system teaches that there are three critical components to real estate investing: systems, relationships and follow-through. Systems, including those that support quality record keeping, are the foundation upon which you build your wealth. Systems that reduce record-keeping errors take time to implement, but once they set the stage for the formation of good business practices, they save you much time and frustration down the road. Remember, too, that relationships can be compromised by poor record-keeping and the action required for follow-through only works when based on quality information!

NOTES:_____

_____

_____

_____

_____

_____

TIP #26: KEEP PERMANENT FILES.

What's worse than not knowing where you put a valuable receipt? Knowing you threw it out!

A lot of people think you are required to keep your tax documents for seven years. In reality, the Canada Revenue Agency rules for document retention vary according to different circumstances. (So do the document retention rules for those of other governing bodies, including various provincial corporation rules, federal corporate rules, labour departments and others. Know before you throw!)

Believe it or not, you are required to keep documents for several departments. All of them require you to keep documentation open for the audit period. The audit period covers any documents claimed in a given year. You can only destroy the documents after a tax audit period is over — and you have to ask permission. (For more on audits, see Tips #59–63.)

Here's where everything gets complicated. Let's say you took a four-year loan that started in March 2006. You will pay interest on that loan to February 2010. The interest paid on that loan will appear on your return in the year 2010. Say you file your return on time in April 2011 and your notice of assessment was mailed April 21, 2010. This loan document must now be held until April 22, 2014.

NOTICE OF REASSESSMENT

For more details on audit periods, see Tip #63. In the meantime, you must also keep in mind notices of reassessment. Going back to the above example, here are two additional scenarios:

1. In November 2010, you get an Amended T-slip from the issuer or the CRA that corrects a previously-provided slip. So you forward that slip to the CRA asking them to amend your return. You get a notice of reassessment on January 29, 2011 to confirm the changes. You now have to wait for three years from this date for all your 2009 tax returns before they are statute barred and ask for permission to destroy your old records.
2. You file your 2011 return in March 2012 and have a capital loss that you can apply to your 2008 return. You make an application to carry

the loss back to 2008. A notice of reassessment is issued for your 2008 return in May 2012. Your three-year wait period now starts from May 2012.

Similar rules apply for property you purchased. It becomes time barred three years from the last date of notice of reassessment after you dispose of your property. The same goes for any equipment purchased.

PERMISSION TO DESTROY

After your audit period is time barred and you are sure you have all the documents, consider asking the CRA for permission to destroy your records.

ACCIDENTAL LOSS

If your documents are accidentally destroyed by fire or flood, contact the CRA. They will visit your place and look at the remnants of the documents. Provide proof of the destroyed documents as you may need that if you are audited and cannot show actual records. If you do not contact the CRA, you risk the chance that all of your expenses will be denied. You can sometimes get around this with proof of an insurance claim, but it is better to contact the CRA and let them see the documents.

 RED FLAG

Avoid suspicion and contact the CRA if your documents are accidentally destroyed.

KEY INSIGHT

The wait period for document retention changes with reassessment, so keep permanent files for information you need (or might need!). Once a property is sold, move that information to the current file as the new wait period begins from the year-of-sale. The same applies to documents related to refinancing. Hold on to them until at least three years after the property is sold!

NOTES:_____
_____
_____
_____

TIP #27: COLOUR-CODE YOUR FILING SYSTEM.

Every time you buy a new property, add four new file folders to your cabinet.

You should put this tip to work before you buy your first property. If it's not already in place, make it a priority now.

This colour-coded filing system was developed by the Real Estate Investment Network and offers a proven way to find specific documents amongst your investment records. It is easy-to-use, is compatible with Canada Revenue Agency rules, and can be used when buying single or multi-family properties.

Let's get started:

1. Buy a filing cabinet that will hold legal-size documents.
2. Buy good-quality file folders in four colours, plus hangers.
3. Every time you buy a new property, add four new file folders.

RED: TENANT INFORMATION

Rental data, move-in and move-out inspection reports, completed tenant questionnaires, lease or rental agreements, a CD of property pictures and all tenant correspondence.

YELLOW: PROPERTY MISCELLANEOUS

General property information, warranties, your master key and all maintenance and inspection information.

BLUE: LEGAL DOCUMENTS

Copy of the offer to purchase, all due diligence documents, survey or title insurance certificates, appraisal and all closing documents. This file should go into the bottom file drawer as it won't be accessed very often.

GREEN: ONGOING MONTHLY RECEIPTS

All receipts related to any expenses on the property. The green folder will get most of the attention and will be opened most often. At the end of each month, gather all of the receipts in a folder and put them in a #10 envelope marked with the month and year. On the outside of the envelope list the company name, the amount paid for each receipt and the classification (office expenses, marketing, maintenance, etc.).

REPLICABLE RECORD

These envelopes now serve as a replicable record of expenses if your computer crashes! No matter how many properties you own, and how good you get at finding and buying new properties, *always* follow your system for filing documents related to each property. A booming market can trick veteran and rookie investors into thinking they don't have to follow their systems. This is a mistake! Market shifts are inevitable and you never want to be looking for documents when you should be taking care of business.

🔘 SOPHISTICATED INVESTOR TIP

Enter all of the receipts in your green files into a QuickBooks, Simply Accounting or Excel-type accounting program at least once a month. Write all of the key details of the receipt on the paper. This will save you countless hours if you are audited. It also provides the kind of information your accountant needs to prepare your return.

NOTES:_____

_____

_____

_____

_____

_____

_____

_____

_____

TIP #28: PROTECT YOURSELF FROM FRAUD.

A robust record-keeping system can deter theft and help with early detection of illegal activities.

Fraudsters are always devising new and elaborate ways to take your assets without your knowledge. In the real estate investment business, you need to be on the look-out for "Look-A-Like Suppliers." Here, the cheater could create a company called something like "Harrow Power and Hydro Ltd." and send you fake invoices for a property you own. Unless you keep a close eye on your expenses, you could pay this invoice without realizing it was a fake. Alternatively, the fraudster may mimic the name of a legitimate company, and instead of paying a legitimate invoice to Harrow Power and Hydro Inc., you or your bookkeeper could write a cheque to a company called Harrow Hydro and Power Ltd. This kind of scam could go on for several months before a problem is identified.

A good record-keeping system is the foundation of fraud prevention. When adopting a system for your real estate investment business, consider the following:

- Complete monthly bank reconciliations on a timely basis. Look for unusual transactions, recognizable names of suppliers and unexpected amounts.
- Review cancelled cheques to ensure that they bear authorized signatures.
- Keep unused cheques in a secure place.
- Monitor credit card statements for unauthorized charges.
- When signing cheques, review the corresponding supplier invoices/ statements to ensure they are authorized. If you use purchase orders, match the supplier invoice/statement with your purchase order number and details.
- Monitor supplier statements for amounts that they state have not been previously paid.
- Practice oversight. Even when others complete much of your bookkeeping activities, conduct spot audits and delegate duties so that one person is not responsible for all of the bookkeeping areas, including writing and signing cheques. Protect your assets by checking on other people's work!

Vigilance against fraudulent activities applies to investor actions, too! Steer clear of lazy investors who advise you to take actions that "trick" lenders or potential co-venturers. You do not want to fake proof of down payment (like borrowing money from a friend or pulling a sizeable cash advance from your credit card to bump up your bank statement), or avoid full disclosure. Ask yourself: What would my lender say to this deal if she knew what I was doing? If she would turn a deal down, you've stepped over the line.

🌀 KEY INSIGHT

Fraud protection begins with you! Bank fraud typically occurs when an investor signs documents that are not true. For example, if you do not intend to move into a property as your principal residence, do not sign documents saying you do intend to live there. Never commit anything that smells of bank fraud—and steer clear of any lender who asks you to sign a false document. Your reputation, your money and your ability to create long-term wealth will all be compromised and you may even spend time in jail.

NOTES:_____

_____

_____

_____

_____

_____

_____

_____

_____

_____

TIP #29: PULL ALL OF THESE RECORD-KEEPING TIPS TOGETHER.

7 Steps to record-keeping success!

1. **Resolve to implement a system that ensures you will find a document the first time you look.**
   a. Take all of your records prior to and including December last year and divide them into a permanent information file and current information file.
   b. Label and put away all files prior to and including December two years ago with current information into a banker's box and place them in a safe place.
   c. Use a banker's box to file last year's documents. Divide them into files labelled "Permanent Information" and "Current Information."

🌀 KEY INSIGHT

Take this information to your accountant early. Do not wait until all of the slips are in.

   d. Set up your filing system by using an accordion file, banker's box or filing cabinet for the current year.
   e. Organize all the paper on your desk and sort it into your filing system.
   f. If you have all your records by date order and have also filed your tax returns on time, ask for permission to destroy records that are seven years old or older.
2. **Create extra time and space by dealing with every paper *once*.**
   a. Have an *IN* basket that is truly an *IN* basket.
   b. Clear the basket each day and respond to each document by:
      i. E-mail or fax.
      ii. Delegate it to a team member by writing a note on it.
      iii. File it in the filing cabinet.
      iv. If you won't need the document again, file it in the recycle bin.
3. **Review and clarify your business goals.**
   a. Why should you get to it?
   b. What are you prepared to do when you get there?
   c. What is the price you have to pay to get it?

    d. Resolve to pay that price in advance.
    e. Do a SWOT analysis: Strengths; Weaknesses; Opportunities; Threats.
      i. Make a list of your strengths and weaknesses.
      ii. Make a list of your opportunities and threats.
      iii. Determine what your focus should be and what's keeping you from getting there.

4. **Prepare an action plan for the current year.**
    a. Prepare your net worth statement now.
    b. Prepare your pro-forma net worth statement at the end of this year.
    c. Write down the action steps required to get there and consider:
      i. The mentors that will help you get there.
      ii. Which professionals will help you get there.
      iii. The kind of education you will need to get there.
      iv. How many new pillars you will be required to add.
      v. Write down the action steps you will need to get there.
      vi. Review your plan from a tax perspective.

5. **Determine your measuring posts.**
    a. How many properties do you need to observe/analyze each week?
    b. How many phone calls need to be made to create the contacts you desire?
    c. How many books do you need to further your research?

6. **Prioritize your action plan.**
    a. Turn your action plan into a TO DO list.
    b. Remind yourself to do it **now** or you will waste valuable time.

7. **Celebrate each success.**
    a. Give yourself a treat for each success.
    b. Thank a person who helped you get there (a bottle of wine for your favourite accountant is a great idea!)
    c. Treat a family member with each success.
    d. Enjoy the journey and have a party.

⊗ SOPHISTICATED INVESTOR TIP

Make every decision as if it will affect the next 20 years of your business.

NOTES:_____
_____
_____

TIP #30: GO ONE STEP FURTHER AND CREATE A VIRTUAL OFFICE.

Store the contents of your filing cabinet on your computer.

Imagine having your office stored on a computer you can access from any secure internet connection. It's easier than you think!

The main benefits to creating a virtual office include accessibility, improved organization and better use of time and money.

1. **Accessibility.**
   You can use the internet to access your information from any secure computer. All of your documents will be stored in a central location with multiple backups.
2. **Improved organization.**
   To get started, all of your documents will need to be scanned and named. This is a time-consuming task, but once you have the folders figured out, upkeep is easy.
3. **Save time and money.**
   A virtual office makes document retrieval faster and more efficient, especially for documents required by multiple users, such as bankers, accountants, co-venturers, the tax department and so forth.

To create a virtual office, follow these steps:

1. **Create a filing system.**
   Use a proven filing system. Review the system outlined in Tip #27 and talk to your accountant about the system they use.
2. **Commit to going paperless.**
   Document scanning takes time. To ease the process, use a good-quality machine with the following:
   a. A document feeder capable of handling multiple widths and thicknesses of paper.
   b. A program that lets you create a generic name for each group of documents you scan. This will save you a lot of time later.
   c. The ability to open up e-mail with documents attached so you only have to enter the location where you want to send the documents.

3. Get help.

Doing all the work yourself will take you away from your core business activities: looking for properties and money. Look for someone who can sort documents, handle the bookkeeping, create the appropriate reports from your data, and manage the Web site so you don't have to worry about security and backup issues.

 **SOPHISTICATED INVESTOR TIP**

Going Virtual
by Navaz Murji, CGA

Fast internet speed is essential. Our office helps clients set up virtual offices and we recommend a download speed of at least 15 mbps and an upload speed of 3 mbps. You also need an efficient computer with a dual-core processor and dual 19-inch screens. The two screens replace your desk as a work area.

We also recommend a commercial scanner that is easy to use and features a good document feeder. We like the roller feeders as they can handle multiple widths of paper, including the variety that receipts are printed on.

NOTES:_____

_____

_____

_____

_____

_____

_____

_____

_____

INVESTOR-IN-ACTION: MARK HEALY AND BETTY ANNE TARINI

Don't guess — know your numbers.

Mark Healy is a busy guy. He operates a thriving retail business with a strong focus on service, oversees a highly successful real estate portfolio and still finds time to answer people's questions about how he got to where he's at. He has less patience for questions about the short cuts he uses to keep track of the paperwork details. That's because Mark doesn't believe in paperwork shortcuts; he believes in systems and checklists.

When Mark, his sister Betty Anne Tarini or another member of his investment team, discovers a way to streamline information and paper flow (whether it's a restaurant receipt or a mortgage document), he creates a system around that method. He then supports that method with a checklist for making sure that bit of information is touched only a minimum amount of times and ends up where it need to go for easy access if it is needed in the future.

With these systems and checklists in place, Mark and his team have more time to build the professional relationships they need to keep their portfolio firmly in the black. He's committed to systems because they strengthen the financial foundation of his real estate investments. This is not about blind faith or empty action. Mark identifies every deposit in his bank account (Tip #20) because he needs to know the details behind every transaction in that bank account. He manages his bank accounts with care (Tip #21), because he wants them to be a good record of money in and out of his business, and they provide data for the first stage of analysis on whether a property is working or not. He raves about the REIN system for colour-coding paperwork (Tip #27), because that system saves him time and money even though he also uses accounting and property management software. When Mark needs a certain document, he knows where it will be. That peace of mind is like money in the bank.

The obvious benefits of good systems aside, real estate investors must take care to only adopt systems that meet two very important criteria. When you're deciding which system to keep and which to toss, take an honest look at the problem that system is supposed to solve. Then ask yourself:

1. **Does it do what you need it to do?** Will this system save you time? Is it proven to work in all market conditions? Don't get fooled by the hype that surrounds systems from outside Canada. Are you buying into

a system — or buying into someone else's portfolio? Are you adopting *proven* practices that successful real estate investors use — or someone else's idea of how your business should run and what your office should look like? Always choose a system backed by a decade of testing in the Canadian market.

2. **Does it increase efficiencies?** "Bring automation to an inefficient business and it will increase the inefficiencies," says Bill Clinton. This is equally true with investment systems. If you build your system or checklists based on an inefficient model, it will not free up your time, it will take time away. Systems take time to put in place, but save time when they're up and running. Duplicate good systems; don't reinvent the wheel.

* * *

Mark Healy knows exactly why he's in the real estate investment business. He's there to create long-term wealth, typically by buying and holding positive cash-flow residential real estate. In that enterprise, cash is king. If a property's not making money, Mark will look at how he can change that around. If change doesn't look possible, or can't happen fast enough, he'll sell the property and move on. A dog's a dog and sometimes a property just turns into a real underperformer, no matter what you do. Get rid of it so you can make your money work harder than you do.

It all sounds good. But Mark separates himself from the rest of the pack because there's bite behind his howl. While some investors struggle with knowing when a property is not adding value to his portfolio, Mark is a disciple of a business philosophy that says you only know what you know. So Mark makes sure he always knows. Cash may be king, but hard numbers makes decisions.

The CEO and owner and GM of Kensington Floors Carpet One, one of Calgary's oldest and most successful flooring companies, Mark works in an industry driven by a strong market for new homes and renovations. With dozens of employees and subcontractors in his employ, he spends his days solving other people's problems. And he's good at it. Kensington Floors has racked up an outstanding collection of sales and customer service awards since Mark took over the business in 2003. He does it all with what he calls "operational systems." "The beauty of operational systems is that they free you up to do what you do best," notes Healy.

In 2003 he also became a director in Connaughty Investment Ltd. Connaughty Investment was started by his father in 1981 and held a few revenue properties. Not long after becoming a director with Connaughty, Mark joined REIN, an organization he'd heard about through a neighbour. Excited about real estate and intrigued by the opportunity to put proven systems to work in his own business, Mark set out to take Connaughty Investment to new heights. Together with his sister, Betty Anne Tarini, he embarked on an aggressive campaign to implement the systems they were learning. They closed on three properties by December 2005 and within four years their portfolio included more than 30 properties and close to 70 doors.

Following a system that begins with the Property Goldmine Score Card (see Appendices), every one of these properties is located in areas with strong economic fundamentals. Committed to each sibling doing what they do best (another system!) Betty Anne finds the deals and handles negotiations and property management. Mark finds the money. He also keeps a lot of the paperwork.

His basic rules of thumb all revolve around the value of good records. Mark knows a lot of things are talked about during the heat of property negotiations, but he never trusts verbal agreements. Instead, he makes sure information is written down so both parties know exactly what's on the table. He's also big on current data. The Sophisticated Investment Binder he learned how to put together in his early days with REIN is designed for lenders and vendors, but also carries the information he needs to manage many of the other relationships his business depends on. Need an asset sheet on any of their properties? Mark has a copy in his binder. Need a Notice of Assessment from the Canada Revenue Agency for a particular year for any shareholder in the company? It's in the binder. Want to compare current and past property taxes? That's in the binder, too. Ditto for quarterly reports, which Mark calls "quarterly" because that's when they're always updated.

He also keeps current information about how every piece of property performs. When the Canadian economy took a nose dive in late 2008, Connaughty lost a long-time tenant who rented one of their houses for foreign employees. The decision to sell the property was made by the cold, hard facts. "We couldn't get $2,100 a month for it anymore, and when we looked at all the numbers, it was obvious that we should not hang onto that property," says Mark.

Access to detailed and current cash flow records further prompted Mark to renegotiate a number of their mortgages in the midst of that economic recession. Those properties were already cash flowing pre-negotiation, but because of the record-low locked-in interest rates that were being offered the new deal cut mortgage payments by about $3,000 a month. That cash infusion happened because Mark had the business numbers he needed to seek a better deal.

Another one of his favourite systems is a colour-coded filing system. He and Betty Anne may handle different parts of the business, but that colour-coded system ensures they both know which folder to pull if they have a query. There have been times when Mark has been asked for additional information by lenders and, while on the phone with them, he has gone to the files, pulled the documents and faxed them to the lender while still talking to the agent.

Those records are also essential to his financial records (Tip #7) and they give Mark the hard data he needs when he has to talk to his accountant about how investment purchases and sales impact tax planning (Tips #47 to #49). For instance, if they have to sell a property and take a profit, Mark needs to know whether that opens opportunities for him and Betty Anne to reduce their tax position by moving up some repair and maintenance costs. Ideally, Mark wants that information well before the next year's taxes are due. In the end, it's all about making sure your information is accurate and up-to-date and then listening to people who know more about taxes than you do.

He's also keen to adopt new technology that makes his systems run more smoothly. In addition to getting the bookkeeping and accounting software his team members need to do their jobs, Mark uses technology to buy him time. His PDA, for example, is programmed to remind him about things he needs to do, well in advance of when they've got to be done. For mortgage renewals, his PDA provides a three-month notice. That time frame can be critical in terms of collecting information and setting up meetings.

It comes down to understanding the financial and emotional cost difference between good decisions and experience. Mark trusts his systems to help him make good decisions. "Good decisions come from experience and experience comes from bad decisions," says Mark. "I look at my systems as a kind of autopilot for my business. If I set the autopilot, I get a good return. There may be times when I don't get the "best" return, but the time and energy I've saved by following a proven path is a reward in itself."

* * *

ACTION STEPS

✓ If you're not sure where to begin putting your systems in place, get help from experienced investors who are willing to share their expertise and experience. Ask your accountant what she wants your records to look like. Hire a bookkeeper who can introduce or follow a record-keeping system that generates the financial records you need.

✓ Take action. Break the big problems down into small solutions and make it your business to solve them.

✓ Be honest about what a lack of systems for your paperwork costs you and refuse to let record-keeping be the bane of any aspect of your real estate investment business.

    – Can't find receipts?

    – Can't remember who you called to repair that faucet three weeks ago?

    – Can't *believe* you missed a bounced rental cheque ?

These are highly fixable problems.

PART 4

EXPENSE REPORTS: KEEP IT REAL (TO KEEP IT DEDUCTIBLE).

TIP #31: RECEIPTS MATTER.

Proof of an expense requires a receipt, an explanation for the expense and proof of payment. Never (ever) trust your memory.

When it comes to the Canada Revenue Agency, the best offense begins with a great defense. Since few novice investors really understand what they need to do when it comes to documenting receipts, we'll walk you through the process of documenting a restaurant meal with your banker.

First, get the receipt from the restaurant. It identifies the number of people and the type of food ordered, plus the date and time. Now write on that receipt the name of the person with whom you dined, as well as the purpose of the meeting. It can be a PR meeting, no problem. Put that receipt into the appropriate file or envelope, and then staple your credit card statement to the file along with a copy of the cheque paid to the credit card company or the bank receipt.

The biggest mistake investors make is when they do not put detailed notes on receipts. When you make a purchase, make sure you document what it's for. Also include notes for your bookkeeper/document filer, instructing her as to where the receipt should be filed and how you want him or her to create a report. To speed up the filing process, only keep relevant receipts. You do not want to pay someone to sort through your business *and* personal receipts!

Also, remember that the CRA can ask you to sort out your receipts and provide proof of your deductions. They will not do your bookkeeping for you.

AIM FOR CONSISTENCY

The CRA looks for inconsistencies that would disallow an expense. Does the receipt include three children's meals? Does the receipt match a credit card entry or cheque?

What happens if you legitimately lose a receipt? You could make the claim with alternate documentation, but a credit card statement on its own is *not* proof of an expense. A cancelled cheque used to pay property taxes on each property you own might work to claim that direct expense.

A bird in the hand is worth two in the bush, and a single envelope of well-documented receipts handed to your accountant before he prepares your tax return is worth a lot more than a drawer-full of receipts you discover three months after your tax return is filed! The fact that you can make late claims does not mean that you should. You do not want to pay more tax than you have to, but you also want to avoid unnecessary accounting fees.

KEY INSIGHT

Every expense disallowed costs you money at your marginal tax bracket, but no entrepreneur or investor needs to be good at handling paper! So do yourself a favour and always make good notes on your receipts, then hire someone to file them for you.

SOPHISTICATED INVESTOR TIP

Keep good notes!
Writing notes on a receipt does not void your deduction, it enhances it.

Take that luncheon receipt, for example, and write on it the name of the project that business luncheon was associated with.

When you keep good notes, stay organized and provide good summaries, you give your accountant what s/he needs to counter CRA questions and audits. Never leave the details to memory alone!

NOTES:_____
_____
_____
_____
_____
_____
_____
_____
_____
_____

TIP #32: EXPENSES ARE REAL, NOT CREATED.

You can deduct bona fide expenses that you incur to earn income, but you will need proper documentation so you can recall the nature and reason for the transaction.

Novice investors often misunderstand the cardinal rule about what constitutes an expense, so let's be clear. To incur an expense, you have to pay for it. Expenses cannot be created, nor implied. Moreover, expenses are typically anything that is reasonable and necessary to earn income, except if it is personal in nature.

PAYING MEMBERS OF YOUR FAMILY

All payments to related parties (family members) must be bona fide transactions. Ask yourself: What would I pay for this transaction if I had to pay a non-related person? You cannot pay your spouse/child more.

The same applies to loans from family. If you borrow $10,000 from your parents, they are helping you out. A normal loan transaction includes periodic payments, interest and security. If you entered a transaction and claimed 5% on your tax return, that could qualify as long as:

a) you wrote a cheque for the interest;
b) your parents declared the interest as income; and
c) the transaction was at fair market value.

You would also be required to repay the loan at an appropriate time, just as if you had borrowed from a bank.

But what about an *implied* expense? Let's say you purchased properties in Edmonton but you live and work in Calgary. Your current employer pays for you to travel to Edmonton, where they expect you to visit clients. If your employer pays for all your expenses, you cannot double dip. Just because you would have to pay these expenses yourself if your employer did not pay them does not make them a business expense. Keep it real!

 RED FLAG

During an audit, you are guilty until you prove you are innocent!

 **KEY INSIGHT**

You do not need a business license to deduct costs. A business license is a matter for municipal taxation. It has nothing to do with earning money.

SOPHISTICATED INVESTOR TIP

Never forget the Canada Revenue Agency has the benefit of hindsight. When you make a decision, you make a judgement based on future expectations. Let's say you plan to take a real estate course or a trip to another town to buy real estate. Your intentions are clear: you will take the course or the trip because you plan to buy real estate to make more money. But what if you change your mind? What if you take the course and then decide real estate investment is not for you? What if you can't find real estate you deem a long-term investment on your trip?

If you are audited, the CRA may say the course you took was not relevant to what you are doing, or deem you had no intention to invest in the area you visited. Because you never made any investments as a result of the original expenditure, the amount is not a deduction.

Also, remember that the CRA's cost to disallow the expense is zero. CRA auditors are on salary. The professional advisors you will have to pay to fight the CRA ruling are not. This underscores the need to keep impeccable records you can quickly retrieve.

NOTES:_____

_____

_____

_____

_____

_____

_____

_____

_____

TIP #33: KNOW HOW TO DEFINE YOUR EXPENSES.

Categorize your expenses correctly (the first time).

There are three kinds of expenses: direct, indirect and personal.

Inexperienced investors may be fooled into thinking that some expenses, and especially those that fall into the Direct Expenses category, are so "obvious" they don't need to work from a list. Don't make that mistake. Lists are critical parts of a sophisticated investment system. They provide an important checklist to guard against error and can be amended at any time.

DIRECT EXPENSES

In the business of renting properties, direct expenses include:

- Property taxes
- Insurance
- Property management fees (paid to third parties)
- Mortgage interest*
- Heat, electricity, water/sewer
- Repairs and maintenance
- All related expenses directly tied to the property (like condo fees, if it's a condo)

🔴 KEY INSIGHT

If you are self-employed, all direct expenses to make the sale are deductible. These include the cost of product, shipping, storage, etc. When in doubt, keep the receipt and make notes on it about the transaction so you can ask your accountant.

💲 SOPHISTICATED INVESTOR TIP

Property management expenses

Always factor in a property management expense, even if you manage the property yourself. Investment properties are similar to a business

Sophisticated Investor Tip continues

---

*Do not confuse this with mortgage payments. The principal portion of the mortgage repayment is not tax deductible.

and your time spent managing that business should be valued. This information will help you down the road: if you eventually decide to have a professional management company run your property, this expense will already be part of your budget — and part of your cash-flow/ROI calculation.

Remember, too, that poor property management is one of the single biggest causes of real estate investment failure! Why? Because quality property management makes an investment work; it keeps satisfied tenants in your buildings, is essential to cash flow, and it gives you time to focus on finding and investing in more properties. Poor management, on the other hand, equals higher stress, sleepless nights and lost relationships.

Once you decide to "go pro," make quality a priority. Whether you contract a full-time service or the services of a manager who helps you market a property and find tenants, look for a company with experience and a good reputation for managing properties through times of peak and low demand.

INDIRECT EXPENSES

Indirect expenses are also used to earn income. These include an office at home that is used solely for business, cell phones, car expenses, courses, gifts, advertising, entertainment, and so on. If you justify and document your reasons why these had to be purchased, you are more likely able to claim them — although they can still be disallowed.

 RED FLAG

Always be prepared to justify and document your indirect expenses, but never assume they will be allowed as deductions. If you own a number of rental properties, the fees to attend a real estate course could be disallowed as an Eligible Capital Expense that must be amortized over several years. This defies logic. But how much are you willing to pay professional advisors to help you "prove" the deduction should stand?

PERSONAL EXPENSES

When it comes to expenses, you must reduce your claim by your personal portion of the expenses.

If you are a commissioned employee and you are required to wear a suit to work, for example, dry cleaning is considered a personal expense. Ergo, it is not deductible. Under that same rationale, if you have a car, you can claim the portion that was used for business purposes.

Employment expenses are a little different. If your employer requires you to have and pay for any work-related expenses, such as an office at home or an assistant to help you, you must get them to fill out a form T2200 so you can claim your employment expenses.

🕐 KEY INSIGHT

Just because the CRA makes it difficult for you to claim expenses does not mean you should avoid claiming them! It is your job to document legitimate expenses and to make sure your expense fits the deduction. After that, it's your accountant's worry.

NOTES:_____

_____

_____

_____

_____

_____

_____

_____

_____

_____

TIP #34: REMEMBER TO CLAIM YOUR INDIRECT EXPENSES.

The most commonly missed indirect expenses are, by definition, not directly linked to your property and it can be more difficult to remember to claim them.

Indirect expenses must be justifiable and documented. That sounds like work! But every dollar you miss as a deduction can cost you more money in income taxes! Once you learn to think of the Canada Revenue Agency as a profit-sharing entity in your earnings, you will see that indirect expenses are worth claiming. To ensure you're not overlooking valid expenses, ask yourself the following questions:

1. Did you buy items for accountants, mortgage brokers and other pillars of your team? These include a bottle of wine at Christmas, gift certificates, etc.
2. Did you entertain any of these pillars/team members/suppliers/tenants/ potential tenants?
3. Did you pay for a condo rider on your home insurance policy?
4. Did your children help you with banking, record-keeping, or making phone calls to your tenants or others on your team?
5. Did you keep track of the use of stationery required to look for properties?
6. Did you need an internet connection to look for properties?
7. Did you need a computer?
8. Did you need an office at home?
9. Did you need to travel to your meetings, to look after properties, etc.?
10. Did you attend seminars?
11. Did you need a cell phone?
12. Did you get professional tax advice, legal advice, etc.?
13. Did you pay your children to help you with internet searches?
14. Did you claim parking charges?
15. Did you maximize income-splitting opportunities? (See Tip #49.)
16. Did you make your mortgage on your home tax deductible? (See Tip #71 and avoid the traps!)

After you've worked through that list of questions, consider making yourself a checklist you can refer to when deciding where specific receipts should go. The checklist can be a good reminder of what you are allowed to claim as an Indirect Expense. If you always pay for parking when you meet with a lender, the checklist can remind you to keep those receipts as a cost of doing business. It is better to keep one properly filed and documented receipt your accountant tells you that you can't claim than to hunt down receipts you did not file.

🕐 KEY INSIGHT

You will have more success in getting deductions for indirect expenses if you own three or more properties. The size of your portfolio provides you with more than a greater revenue base, it can also demonstrate that you are a serious investor with an enterprise that justifies and requires more expenses than an investor just starting out.

NOTES:_____

_____

_____

_____

_____

_____

_____

_____

_____

TIP #35: REPAIRS AND IMPROVEMENTS ARE NOT THE SAME THING WITH RESPECT TO A RENTAL PROPERTY.

Property improvements do not get the same tax deductions as repairs.

With a few specific exceptions, you can generally write off 100% of repairs to a rental property. Improvements are a whole other story — which is exactly why you need to understand the differences and act accordingly!

Since you get to write off 100% of repairs, the tax savings are substantial. If you are in the top bracket and spend $10,000, you would save $3,900 to $5,100 on taxes, depending on the province in which you live. Improvements are an addition to a building, which means you must amortize the cost over a longer period of time. In the year of acquisition on many buildings, you get 2% and then 4% on a declining balance method. In short, if you spend $10,000 on your property, you may get to deduct $200 in the first year and $390 in the second year, and so on. Your tax savings depends on your marginal bracket. So if you are at 42%, your saving in Year 1 would be $84. That's peanuts! (For more on the marginal tax bracket, see Tip #46 and Tip #47.)

REVIEW THE RULES

With the Canada Revenue Agency wanting to call many repairs improvements, and real estate investors wanting the opposite, investors need to make sure they understand the rules. Briefly summarized, they are:

1. An improvement is a betterment to the property; and
2. A repair puts the property back to its original condition.

From the CRA's perspective, the key words are *betterment* and *original*. This means that a new basement suite in a rental property is an improvement, but installing new carpet to replace old carpet is a repair.

AN ISSUE OF TIMING

The tax department also uses "timing" to decide whether you are making a repair or an improvement. Replacing the roof with exactly the same materials soon after you buy a property is usually deemed an improvement in the CRA's opinion. Replace the roof six months later because of a leak you were unaware of despite your due diligence at the time of purchase, and you are likely to be allowed to deduct the repair.

🕐 KEY INSIGHT

Quality properties attract quality tenants. Since real estate investment is typically meant to be a long-term wealth-building strategy, updating units right after purchase is an investment in your business. That's why sophisticated investors are more apt to invest in their property than to make decisions based on tax avoidance.

To put this insight into action, sophisticated investors learn to picture their property as if it was a retail store, like a video store, for example. To make sure your video store attracts the kind of clients who will keep you in business for a long time, you need to give those clients good reasons to shop at your store (and not the competition's!).

For more background on the importance of quality tenants, review *Real Estate Investing in Canada* and *97 Tips for Canadian Real Estate Investors*.

💲 SOPHISTICATED INVESTOR TIP

For more detail on Capital vs. R&M expenses, see the CRA's interpretation bulletin IT-128R. It reviews the differences between what the tax department defines as an enduring benefit, maintenance or betterment, integral part of a separate asset, relative value, differences based on an acquisition and anticipation of a sale.

NOTES:_____

_____

_____

_____

_____

_____

_____

_____

_____

Tip #36: Purchase your car personally.

Claim the business portion of your vehicle expenses.

Greenhorn investors often get very excited about industry chatter that says you can buy or lease a vehicle and claim it as a business expense. This chatter is misguided! It is often not advisable to purchase or lease an automobile in your corporation, since the limits and standby benefits may be onerous. First, they limit the cost of the vehicle to $30,000, plus HST (PST and potentially GST). This means that if you buy a vehicle for $50,000, for capital cost allowance (CCA is also interpreted as depreciation), your maximum cost is $30,000, plus sales taxes. Your CCA is 30% on a declining balance method with half in the year of purchase. However, the CRA will charge you a benefit for having access to a $50,000 vehicle.

Buy your car personally

To recover some of the costs associated with using your car for business, claim the expenses on the use of your car. This is calculated on the mileage used for business purposes. Travelling to and from your office is not considered a business expense. But if you travel to see clients and your rental properties, or if you are a commissioned employee or a tradesperson who travels from various job sites and you are not reimbursed by your employer, you should claim the business portion of your vehicle expenses. Certain restrictions exist, particularly where you personally own less than three properties.

Keep a distance log

Date	Start Location	End Location	Start kms	End kms	Driven	Notes
1-Oct	Home	Rental property 1	65344	65365	21	Collect Rent
1-Oct		Prop 2	65365	65380	15	Collect Rent
1-Oct		Prop 3	65380	65390	10	Collect Rent
10-Oct	Home	Personal	65390	65650	260	
10-Oct	Home	Seminar	65650	65699	49	
11-Oct	Home	Personal	65699	65730	31	
12-Oct	Work	Bank	65730	65750	20	Set up Line of Credit

Do I really need to keep a distance log?

The short answer (and only answer) is Yes. The information noted in a distance log like the one noted here takes time to document. But this kind of log is an essential component of a systems-approach to the real estate investment business, which advocates best management practices that put proactive business strategies into action.

SOPHISTICATED INVESTOR TIP

A decision about what kind of car to buy is not a tax decision. It is a personal expense and should be treated that way. Since you can only deduct a portion of your car expenses and there are upper limits, this is a personal decision and should be treated that way.

NOTES:_____

_____

_____

_____

_____

_____

_____

_____

_____

TIP #37: YOU CAN DEDUCT FINANCING COSTS.

There is a right way to deduct these costs. Do it the wrong way and it could cost you interest, plus penalties!

The costs related to securing financing for a property are deductible. But they are deductible over a period of time, not all at once.

Typical costs include bank charges, CMHC fees and mortgage broker charges. Novice investors mistakenly deduct these expenses as they are incurred. That makes them relatively easy for the Canada Revenue Agency to spot. If they are missed, but identified a few years after the fact, the CRA could charge substantial interest.

 **KEY INSIGHT**

When it comes to expense reports, it's easy to get caught up in the details of quality record-keeping systems. Systems are important. But never forget that relationships and follow-through are also essential components of successful real estate investing. Timely deductions of financing costs are a good example of why you need to develop a business relationship with an accountant who understands real estate investing. When advice is based on experience, the follow-through is easy.

NOTES:_____

_____

_____

_____

_____

_____

_____

_____

_____

_____

TIP #38: A LOAN CAN BE INTEREST DEDUCTIBLE.

You can deduct the interest on a loan if it was used to earn income.

Keep it real. If you have a bona fide loan used to earn qualifying income (there are a variety of exceptions), you can claim the loan interest as a tax deduction. For this to happen, you must document the following:

1. The loan must be real. It cannot be an implied loan from yourself, or be fictitious.
2. Interest must ultimately be paid.
3. The loan must be documented with a rate of interest, terms of repayment, an amortization period and a term for the duration of the loan.
4. The funds should be traced directly to the investment, which must be real.

Most interest paid on monies borrowed for investment purposes are tax deductible *at this time* (the Canada Revenue Agency is tinkering with the rules). It is interesting to note that most monies borrowed for the stock market are tax deductible, even though some of the stocks have a limited potential to earn dividend income. When it comes to real estate, the CRA has tried to limit the amount of interest so that you cannot get a loss from a property!

THE PAY-OFF STRATEGY

Overall, your objective is always to pay off loans where the interest is not deductible for tax reasons. If you borrow $100,000 and your interest rate is 6%, your interest payments would be $6,000 (assuming it's compounded annually, and more if compounded semi-annually). If the interest is tax deductible, your loan just got cheaper by the amount of taxes you save based on your marginal tax bracket. So, if your marginal tax rate is 22%, your tax savings are $6,000 x 22% = $1,320. If you are in a 42% tax bracket, your savings would be $2,520.

HOW DO YOU MAKE THE LOAN TAX DEDUCTIBLE?

Traceability is one of the factors that make a loan deductible; typically, the CRA follows the direct flow of money. If you borrow $100,000 and deposit it in your lawyer's trust account and use it for a down payment on rental property, it becomes directly traceable.

If you take the $100,000 and put it in your personal bank account, things might change. As long as you write a cheque on the same day for $100,000 to buy a property and it clears the bank the same day, you probably won't have a problem. But this gets messy if there are other transactions.

Let's say you pay your personal credit card bills for $10,000 out of that $100,000. Now only 90% of that $100,000 deposit is directly traceable, so that's the amount you may be limited to in terms of deducting interest.

If you're not yet convinced you need separate bank accounts for your personal and business transactions, review the tips related to bank accounts in Part 2. If you adopt a system that values quality record keeping, then you will need to separate your business and personal bank accounts. In addition to making it easier for you to monitor account activity and to keep your personal and business transactions separate, different accounts ease traceability by making it easier to identify the funds moving in and out of those accounts.

 **KEY INSIGHT**

1. You can only deduct the interest you pay.
2. Your loans must be bona fide, not implied.
3. Do not mingle proceeds of a loan you received for investment purposes with other funds.

NOTES:_____

_____

_____

_____

_____

_____

_____

_____

TIP #39: DOCUMENTATION IS KEY TO DEDUCTING INTEREST.

Make sure your payments can be traced to an eligible investment.

The rules related to interest deductibility can be confusing, but a recent Supreme Court of Canada decision offers some clarification. In January 2009, the Supreme Court confirmed in the Lipson case instances where the interest charges on mortgages for a rental property itself are deductible, as is the interest from other loans, provided certain conditions are met.

One of these conditions relates to maintaining the ability to trace the source of the borrowed funds to an eligible investment. Structuring your financial affairs correctly may allow you to deduct more of your interest costs, thus saving more money.

More specifically, Canadians are allowed to deduct interest charges where they use a line of credit, second mortgage, or separate loan to pay for a portion of a property's deposit or various operating expenses related to the property. These expenses can include repairs, utilities and property taxes. The key is being able to trace the payments from the line of credit to the property. Ideally, a separate line of credit is used wholly for investment purposes. Where you require a line of credit for personal use, this should be done with a separate account. This ensures you do not mix amounts spent on your vacation or big-screen TV with those related to your investments.

A variety of financial institutions have debt products which allow you a total amount of debt and then divide this total into multiple accounts you have created. Over time, it may also be possible to restructure your debt so that even otherwise non-deductible interest can be converted into fully deductible interest. To make sure you can take advantage of deductible interest, talk to your tax advisor about what you can do to deduct as much of your interest as possible — and in a method that is acceptable to the CRA.

🌑 KEY INSIGHT

A separate line of credit for investing is the simplest way to track funds in and out of that account and it will make it easy for you to determine their deductibility, possibly using the Canada Revenue Agency's criteria for allocating payments.

TIP #40: CLOSING DOCUMENTS INCLUDE ITEMS WITH UNIQUE TAX CONSEQUENCES.

Claim your deductions and avoid audit exposure by understanding that some closing costs are treated differently.

When you examine the statement of adjustment and trust statement, both of which are closing documents for a property, you will find a handful of items that have unique tax consequences because they are treated differently from normal closing costs, which are capitalized.

Some of these items will be immediately included or deducted from your income, while others will be capitalized and deducted over time or only on sale of the property. The tax differences are frequently missed by investors, which leaves investors exposed to audit issues or means they miss deductions they could otherwise claim.

⑤ SOPHISTICATED INVESTOR TIP

Review Closing Costs
by George Dube, CA

Some of the items with unique tax consequences include closing costs such as legal fees, real estate commissions and land transfer taxes (which go by other names in provinces outside Ontario). These are capitalized with the property, meaning they are included as part of the cost of the property.

If the property is considered a capital property for tax purposes (typically the case where the property is held for long-term rental), the portion of these costs allocated to the building will be amortized over time with the building. The portion allocated to land is not allowed to be amortized and thus will only serve to reduce the capital gain (or increase a capital loss) on ultimate disposition.

Fees paid with respect to financing a property are generally capitalized and deducted over a period of five years.

Adjustments are frequently made on account of property taxes, last month's rent, rent for a period of the month and utilities, for example. The last month's rent and the remaining rent for the month will typically be paid to the purchaser and included as a deposit and income, respectively.

Property tax and utility adjustments may generate either an expense or income to the purchaser.

TIP #41: SEGREGATE PRINCIPAL AND INTEREST FOR MORTGAGE PAYMENTS.

Only the interest is deductible!

Remember those financial statements we talked about understanding back in Tip #6? When you look at your cash flow statements, you'll see that mortgage payments comprise a large portion of your expenses. It makes sense that you will want to reduce the effective cost of a property by claiming as large a tax deduction as possible.

Novice investors often want to treat the entire mortgage payment as deductible. That's not possible, since **only the interest component of your payments is deductible**.

To guard against an inaccurate claim, separate the principal and interest portions of your payments in your accounting records. This can be done on an annual basis. While doing this, compare your annual mortgage statements with your amortization table to ensure accuracy, or at least reasonableness.

For example: Say a property costs $100,000 and you allocate $75,000 towards the building and $25,000 towards the land. If you finance 100% of the property at a 5% interest rate, you ultimately deduct the following: a) interest expense of 5% per year; and b) amortization on $75,000 of the building.

What you cannot deduct is the cost of the land. From the perspective of the principal payments, being allowed to deduct the principal in full means you would, in fact, double count your available deductions. In other words, you would deduct $75,000, plus $100,000 plus the interest, all for a building only costing $100,000. You can rest assured the Canada Revenue Agency is not quite that generous.

🅢 SOPHISTICATED INVESTOR TIP

Sophisticated investors take lenders a copy of their Sophisticated Investment Binder with a mortgage application already completed. If the lender transfers that information to his own form, read all the fine print before you sign it. Once it's signed, you've authorized a credit search. Some forms also include hidden clauses with other implications. Exercise due diligence to avoid unwelcome surprises.

TIP #42: KNOW WHAT TO DO IF YOU'VE MISSED A TAX DEDUCTION OR TAX CREDIT.

Taxes are a cost of doing business. You should pursue an adjustment if there's been an error or omission.

It can be agonizing to realize you missed a tax deduction or tax credit for a prior year. Rest assured it is better to notice an error or omission than never know you paid too much in taxes, since you can pursue an adjustment from the Canada Revenue Agency!

On a personal basis, the CRA will often allow you to file a request for a change to your tax return for up to 10 years. This process begins with a general letter, or by filling out a specific form. Although the CRA is not technically required to go back that far, the agency frequently does so, when asked.

If your adjustment relates to a corporation or other entity, a request for three years is not usually a problem.

CONSIDER YOUR OPTIONS

Investors should always think about whether the tax credit or deduction is worth it, since a request to revisit a file reopens the tax year(s) to audit. It also extends the time period under which the CRA can audit the particular year. This means you won't want to ask for a change for relatively minor amounts.

Increasing the likelihood of further scrutiny or an audit may have good, bad or neutral consequences for your investment business. But do be forewarned that related transactions will clearly be subject to a rigorous review, since the CRA will need to take a thorough look at the reasons you have requested a change.

ⓢ SOPHISTICATED INVESTOR TIP

Never confuse the need to make money with tax avoidance.

When you're calculating income and expenses, pay attention to positive cash flow. Negative cash-flow properties take money from you every month and that will impact your business—and lifestyle! Making matters worse, negative cash flow properties don't just drain you financially, they'll suck you

Sophisticated Investor Tip continues

dry *emotionally*, too. Still not convinced? Ask yourself: How many negative cash flow properties can I afford to own before I go broke?

So what should you do when real estate promoters try and sell you a negative cash flow property with the "guarantee" of rents that will dramatically increase? Look at What's Behind The Curtain.

First, there are no guarantees in the real estate investment business. Second, the investment fundamentals show us that you will need to increase rent to reverse a negative cash flow and that can't happen unless the market can support rental increases.

Here's where due diligence is critical. If the property has a negative cash flow because of vacancy issues, you must use market fundamentals (not hopes and dreams!) to determine whether that can be turned around. See the Appendices and review the property score card and REIN property analyzer form to make sure your due diligence is on track.

NOTES:_____

_____

_____

_____

_____

_____

_____

_____

_____

_____

🅐 INVESTOR-IN-ACTION: RUSSELL WESTCOTT

Always ask yourself: How can I make what I do better?

Many novice real estate investors want to take investment action without being honest about what's at stake. They get caught up in the emotional side of the deal and fall into the tax traps noted in Tip #11. Others neglect some of the basic and essential aspects of investing — for instance making sure your financial house is in order and stays that way. Others foolishly try to invest without spending the time and money to ensure they have experienced professionals on their team who can help them navigate the world of bookkeeping, accounting, taxes and legal structures.

Russell Westcott is different. He's now all about doing things the right way and insists that approach saves him time and money and helps him avoid frustration. However, it wasn't always this way and it has been a painful learning experience for Russell, as you'll find out through his story.

It is important to read Russell's story and realize that by the time he wrote his Seven-Year Life Plan at the age of 33, Russell was awash in trouble. A university graduate, he was emotionally and physically exhausted from working so hard. He was also financially exhausted from spending more money than he made. Instead of being happy about what his future held, Russell was stressed. He was also honest enough with himself to realize that he was headed for disaster. He will be the first to tell you it's tough to have to change life direction mid-course. He'll also tell you it's worth it.

More than anything, Russell's story is about recognizing that, no matter what you believe your circumstances are, you are never "stuck." You can always change the path you're on. All you need is the desire to change, then find the support to make it happen. Small changes accumulate and lead to major directional changes. Russell lives by the creed, "If you aren't happy with your results or your life, change your actions so you are."

For Russell, the ability to take action is rooted in his determination to seek solutions to problems and not get hung up on the emotions that surround the problems themselves. He urges other investors to apply that same strategy to every business problem they encounter. Figure out what you're really afraid of. Analyze it. Solve it. Move on.

* * *

Russell Westcott had a problem. During a trip home from Vancouver to rural Saskatchewan in 2001, the 33-year-old put pencil to paper and tried to figure out what he was doing wrong. The financial picture he painted was downright ugly. On the one hand, he looked like a guy who had it all. Armed with a degree in commerce, Russell was working at the Western Canadian headquarters of a global dairy business. Educated, enthusiastic and highly coachable, his career trajectory was trending up. Behind the outward signs of success, however, Russell was treading deep water and he was a long way from the safety of the shore.

Black, white and red all over, his financial bottom line told the real story: Russell was spending more money than he was making. He had a super-hot convertible car he couldn't afford. He was paying for vacations beyond his means. "I had too much, too soon and my lifestyle was economically unsustainable."

Determined to make real-life changes, Russell wrote out a Seven-Year Life Plan that included financial goals and long-term vision. Fresh awareness of his economic circumstances also prompted a meeting with an investment fund salesman and that led him to read the best-selling book *Rich Dad, Poor Dad* by Robert Kiyosaki. Captivated by the potential to create long-term wealth with real estate investment, he started reading more and took some seminars. "I probably spent $30,000 on real estate education in the early days. Some of it was a complete waste of time as it didn't teach anything that worked in Canada. However, I took what I could learn and put it into action. I was starting to understand that I didn't actually have to create a system on my own. To be successful, what I needed to do was learn from others who were already doing what I wanted to do right here in Canada."

In late 2002, Russell flew to Edmonton to take one of REIN's weekend programs. He bought his first cash-flowing investment property early the next year. Determined to buy one property a month, he spent his days working on his job and another 20-plus hours a week learning about real estate investment and building his real estate investor network. Looking back, he figures he was working 60 hours a week and getting smarter all the time.

In December 2004, Russell left his great job as a national marketing manager to immerse himself in real estate full time, investing and teaching others how to invest. He had close to two years' experience with his investment systems by then and his modus operandi was all about taking informed action. "I had this hockey coach who used to tell us, 'You've got to shoot the puck.' Real estate investment is the same thing. Once you've learned what to do, you've got to go out and do it. Investing theory is a waste if you don't put it into action."

Let the Fundamentals Work for You

That same focus on informed action guided Russell's approach to the financial management side of his business. Deliberately seeking opportunities to surround himself with successful investors, Russell looked for ways to emulate their systems. In the early days, that sometimes meant asking investors if they could refer him to a good bookkeeper, accountant, lawyer or property manager. And names weren't necessarily enough. Before adding individuals to his investment team, Russell asked them about their own portfolios. "I wanted to work with people who were doing what I was doing."

Russell figures he was buyihg two properties a month, all townhouse-style condominiums, by early 2007. One hundred per cent of them were in economically strong Western Canadian regions and Russell was basing his decisions not on emotions, but on whether a region had future potential or not.

On the upside, Russell was now an experienced real estate investor, so he used the period of "market correction" that began in September 2008, to consolidate his portfolio, buying out some partners and adding others. But he never changed his basic rules of engagement. Even when an economic recession was confirmed, Russell stuck by his best business management practices: he likes to check his on-line bank statements every morning and reviews them more closely every Friday. "It's a habit I got into and it really helps me stay on top of things," says Russell.

He also hasn't changed his staunchness about making buy/sell decisions based on market fundamentals. Russell likes his properties to have at least two bedrooms, comparable market rents and be located in good complexes with good tenant profiles and good condo boards. In 2009, as in 2007, he will write an offer without seeing a property, but only because he trusts the information he gets from a real estate agent who specializes in investment property — and knows what Russell wants. He also knows he has a trusted team of professionals to back him up.

That trust is no substitute for due diligence. Russell's offers always stipulate a conditional time frame that gives him time to get from Vancouver to wherever the property is located. "This is a business decision and my system stipulates due diligence."

He also continues to stand by his decision to have all of the properties in his portfolio professionally managed. Quality property management is an ongoing business concern, but it's essential to Russell's bigger plan, so he's always on the lookout for ways to upgrade his property management. "I have a very full life and quickly learned that I don't make any money managing properties on a day-to-day basis. I want to focus on the invest-ment side, plain and simple," says Russell.

That decision to focus on what he does best and let the professionals do what they do best is essential to sophisticated real estate investment, says Russell. He tells other investors to find the three things they do best and then leave the rest to others. Russell makes the deals, finds the money and manages the relationships he has with other professionals. (In other words, he manages the managers.) These professionals are charged with finding the properties, keeping the books, devising the tax strategies, pre-paring the legal documents, finding the tenants, managing the properties, and so on.

And what does Russell tell people who "think" they may want to invest in real estate? "Take the Canadian ACRE program and pick up a good book like *Real Estate Investing in Canada*. For a $35 investment in the book you'll discover whether real estate investment is in your future or not. If you're in, then you'll need to take that ACRE course and you'll need to think ahead."

He also reminds them to never forget to only take risks they can live with. As long as your focus is on informed action, that approach opens way more doors than it closes, says Russell. Never let anyone manipulate you into doing something you're not comfortable with.

*   *   *

ACTION STEPS

✓ Be honest and ask yourself: "Are my real estate investment records clear and updated monthly, which helps me make informed decisions?" If not, identify the real problem: is it that you have too much chaos and cannot retrieve key documents when you need them? Are you missing key receipts, from donuts to gas, to tenant acknowledgements? Have you not received clear instructions from your real estate accountant regarding what you can and cannot claim as legitimate expenses? Talk to three real estate investors you admire and ask if you can meet with them to talk about ways to improve your accounting and record keeping systems.

✓ Ask sophisticated real estate investors if they can refer you to a good bookkeeper, accountant, lawyer or property management company.

✓ Are members of your real estate investment team interested in attending real estate investment events that offer a real educational bang for their buck? Do not wait for them to come to you. Send them information you think they should have.

PART 5

THE FACTS ABOUT TAX: HOW TO PUT YOUR KNOWLEDGE OF CANADIAN TAXES TO WORK.

TIP #43: FILE AND PAY YOUR TAXES ON TIME.

It's not your money, so don't be fooled into thinking there is a benefit to filing or paying your taxes late.

Interest and penalties for late filing and paying late are not tax deductible. In fact, paying late attracts escalating fines. These penalties can be substantial — and compounded!

Savvy investors know they can borrow money for a lot less than these late fees tally. They also recognize that avoiding extra payments to the Canada Revenue Agency is the easiest way to reduce taxes!

 **KEY INSIGHT**

We've said it before and we'll say it again: Reducing taxes has a strong emotional pull on the hearts of most Canadians. Well, real estate investing for long-term wealth creation is not a matter of the heart! As a business person, it's your job to make money and avoid paying more tax than you should. Filing and paying taxes on time is one of the simplest examples of what a savvy business person does to cut unnecessary costs.

NOTES:_____

_____

_____

_____

_____

_____

_____

_____

_____

TIP #44: KNOW YOUR TAX DEADLINES.

Penalties for late payments are based on the amount payable.

Your personal tax return is due April 30, unless you are self-employed, when the due date is June 15. But if you owe money, your taxes are due April 30. As a general rule of thumb, avoid problems — and penalties — by sticking to April 30 as the tax deadline.

Novice investors may think you can file a return late if you expect a refund. The truth is more complicated, so be careful.

1. If you get a refund and you are late in filing, the CRA does not have to be quick about getting your refund to you. The CRA tends to be more lenient about late filing with personal taxes and much less so with GST and corporate taxes. Regardless, file your return on time.
2. If you do get into an audit situation, and do owe taxes, penalties on the amount payable will apply for late filing.

Here's what that looks like in action: If your personal tax return shows an amount owing of more than $3,000 ($1,800 if you are a resident of Quebec) in either of the past two years, you are required to make tax installments due on March 15, June 15, September 15 and December 15, assuming your taxes for the current year will be at least $3,000 (or $1,800 for Quebecers). The best way to make these installments is to use online banking, as the CRA has a habit of applying the tax installments to the wrong year. If that happens, you will have to spend some time making sure the error is corrected. To guard against installments being applied to the wrong year, experienced real estate investors will record their social insurance number (or business number, for corporations) and note the period and purpose of the payment on the front of the cheque in the memo field. Others may send the cheque with a cover letter. Most times they do not read the cover letter. But be forewarned. These can still be applied to the wrong year, so vigilance is critical.

 RED FLAG

Watch your statements of account to ensure that the balances in the CRA's records reconcile to your records. An error, even if it's not yours, can still cost you.

TAX PAYABLE AND PAYMENTS

The CRA assumes your tax payable for the current year will be the same as last year. In the first year you are required to make installments, your installments may be spread over two periods, with payments due on September 15 and December 15. The following year, you will need to also make payments on March 15 and June 15. You will get notices of the amounts once — and you should generally follow the amount they ask for. Keep in mind though, that there are three acceptable methods to calculate the installments owing for the year, so you can choose what works best for you.

If you own your own corporation, you are required to make installments if your taxes payable are in excess of $3,000. The installments may be due quarterly, or monthly, depending on your situation. Generally speaking, you are required to make the final payment for the balance of your taxes two months after year-end if you run a passive business or your corporation has taxable income in excess of $500,000. If it is an active business, the final payment generally must be made three months after year-end if the income is below the small business limit. Corporations have to file tax returns six months after year-end. Since taxes are due two or three months after year-end, you will want to work with an accountant who files returns within that time frame.

 SOPHISTICATED INVESTOR TIP

The Early Bird . . .
by George Dube, CA

Good work takes time and your accountant needs to have all of the information he needs roughly one month before a deadline.

Where time does not permit for the completion of the financial statements and tax returns within the two- or three-month deadline, your accountant may be able to make a reasonable estimate of taxes owing. This avoids additional interest and penalties — and underlines the value of a good working relationship with your accounting professional.

 RED FLAG

Late filers are flagged and your chances of audit may be higher. See Tip #62.

Don't Worry, Be Informed

Novice investors may be overwhelmed by the need to meet tax deadlines and keep up to date on tax installments, especially since you may be on the hook for errors that arise from sheer confusion. This is another argument for working with an accounting professional who also understands the real estate investment business. Learn to see your accountant as a member of your team with specialized knowledge. Whereas novice investors may lament their annual accounting bill, experienced investors are often willing to pay a little extra to people who they trust can help them create long-term wealth with real estate investment.

 **KEY INSIGHT**

All payments to the Canada Revenue Agency are taxes. Act accordingly! If you can avoid late penalties and interest, you cut your taxes.

NOTES:_____
_____
_____
_____
_____
_____
_____
_____
_____

TIP #45: GET YOUR EMPLOYEE STATUS DEFINITIONS STRAIGHT.

Are you employed, self-employed or a personal service corporation? The CRA will want to know.

It may be obvious that you are self-employed as a real estate investor. But what about the people who work for you? Everyone should be clear about how these roles are legally defined, as it does impact taxes.

An *employee* is someone who works for a corporation or other person/ entity and gets CPP, EI and taxes deducted at source. If an employee is required to pay for her own expenses, then she would get a T2200 form and would be allowed to make certain limited deductions on her tax returns. She may also be eligible to get GST rebates on the expenses she had to pay.

A *self-employed person* is one who works for herself as a proprietor or through a corporation. Some employers may hire self-employed contractors to avoid paying CPP, EI and some other payroll expenses that companies have to pay. Employers may tell employees they can make additional deductions if they are self-employed. This warrants more discussion with your accountant, since you want to avoid future problems. The real issue often boils down to control, although a variety of factors are looked at to determine whether an employee or independent contractor relationship exists.

Among other questions, ask yourself:

1. Who controls the hours of service?
2. How are they paid? Frequency same as employees?
3. Do they have any risk? Is there a chance this business will lose money? Is it simply a briefcase and business card?
4. Can they work for the competition?
5. Do they have multiple customers?
6. Can they delegate their work to other employees?

Some employers ask employees to incorporate in order to protect themselves from certain audit risks related to the employee/independent contractor issue. If that happens, the corporation may be considered a *personal service corporation.*

With deductions severely limited when you are considered a personal service corporation, and your taxes higher than some corporations, there can still be tax advantages to this set-up when compared to earning the income personally. If your corporation is considered a "normal" corporation, the tax advantages may be significantly greater, including the types of deductions you are allowed.

Recognize who's on your team

The specifics of employee status definitions aside, sophisticated investors recognize that all of their employees are members of their respective investment teams, regardless of whether they are paid employees, self-employed contractors or operate under a personal service corporation. Whether they are property managers, bookkeepers or provide office support, each needs to be empowered to do what they do best. Oversight of the various responsibilities, however, is your job and this is where your systems approach to record keeping and traceability comes into play, big time. Clear directives make it easier to trace actions, identify problems and work towards continuous improvement.

 RED FLAG

Employers, including some government departments, sometimes mandate individuals set up a corporation as a provision of "employment." Talk to your lawyer and accountant before you agree to these terms.

DID YOU KNOW?
Declaration of Conditions of Employment
If your employee plans to deduct employment expenses from his or her employment income, the CRA requires that you complete a T2200 form, Declaration of Conditions of Employment. The employee is not required to file this form, but they need to keep it in case the CRA asks to see it.

Here is a quick look at how your answers to specific questions could impact your employee's tax situation if he or she claims something different from what's on the form. The detail the CRA expects also shows how important it is to document expenses!

Questions on the T2200 include:

- Did this employee's contract require the employee to pay his or her own expenses while carrying out the duties of employment?
- Did this employee receive a motor vehicle allowance?
- Did this employee receive a repayment of the expenses he or she paid to earn employment income? If yes, indicate the amount and type of expenses that were:
  - Received upon proof of payment
  - Charged to the employer, such as credit card charges
  - Included on the employee's T4 slip
- Did you require this employee to pay other expenses for which the employee did not receive any allowance or repayment?
- Did you require this employee under a contract of employment to use a portion of his or her own home for work? (The work space must be where the employee mainly (more than 50% of the time) does his or her work OR used only to earn the employment income and also used on a regular basis and continuous basis for meeting clients or customers.) You are also asked:
  - Did you repay this employee for any of the expenses?
  - If yes, indicate the type of expenses and amount you did or will repay.

Want to take a closer look?

Learn to navigate the CRA Web site, www.cra-arc.gc.ca, or Google: Declaration of Conditions of Employment, Canada.

NOTES:_____

_____

_____

_____

_____

_____

_____

_____

_____

_____

TIP #46: UNDERSTAND THE CONCEPT OF MARGINAL TAXES.

To pay more tax, you need to make more money.

The same people who think successful businesses do not pay tax (see Tip #1!) may try to tell you there is a point when you should stop working because you pay more in taxes than you earn. Nothing could be further from the truth. Indeed, marginal tax rates exist to ensure there is no disincentive to making money. Think about it: governments are partners in our money-making activities. Since they make money when you make money, they do not like to participate in employment or investment activities where you lose money or are simply "exploring" ways to make money.

The numbers relating to marginal tax rates are different in every province and change almost every year. Annual calculations for the marginal tax rate can be found on provincial Web sites. Look yours up.

To illustrate the concept of how your marginal tax rate affects you, consider the following figures as if they were used by an actual province:

Marginal tax rate for Province X

Income earned	Tax rate
$0 – $10,000	0%
$10,001 – $40,000	22%
$40,001 – $100,000	32%
$100,000 +	42%

Once you reach a threshold, you pay the tax differential on the additional income only. Using this chart, we see that someone who earns $11,000 would have tax payable of $220. Under the same chart, the most tax you will pay is 42%.

 **KEY INSIGHT**

Planning with your marginal tax rates

Talk to your accountant about calculating your marginal tax. You will need all of the information that can be reasonably estimated about your tax situation for various sources of income and deductions that are available you.

Key Insight continues

Often, this will be discussing the changes in the amounts of income and deductions compared to the prior year.

Once you know your taxable income, you need information about the planning points you are considering with your types of income. For example, if you are looking at the impact of receiving additional interest income, dividends, making RRSP deductions or selling property in the current or future year. Typically, these are categorized in three classes:

- Fully taxable income
- Dividends
- Capital gains

Your marginal tax rate in each category depends on how much money you earned and the deductions plus that you claimed.

In Alberta, for example, rental income is fully taxable and the highest marginal tax rate is 39%. (This means you keep 61% of income from rent when you are at the highest personal tax bracket. Note that there can be some idiosyncracies to the brackets where benefits such as old age security or employment insurance are "clawed back" by the government.)

The marginal tax rate is different for dividends and capital gains.

Calculate your options
Wise real estate investors use marginal tax data in two ways:

1. To calculate how much tax you'll pay on extra income (and how much you'll pay if you reach a higher bracket).
2. To figure out how much tax you will save if you increase your deductions.

NOTES:_____

_____

_____

_____

_____

_____

_____

_____

_____

TIP #47: PUT YOUR MARGINAL TAX RATE TO WORK.

Use your marginal tax rate to calculate the cost/benefit of discretionary income.

How do you use your marginal tax rate to make decisions? Let's say you earn a passive income of $100,000. You are retired, but get an offer to earn $50,000 a year. To calculate your marginal tax rate using the table noted in Tip #43, take the $50,000 you could be earning and subtract 42% ($21,000). If you take the $50,000 job, you will net $29,000. Now ask yourself, "Do I want the job for $29,000?

You would weigh similar information if deciding to move to a different city or country with a different marginal tax rate.

Marginal rates can help pensioners, people with two jobs and those with investment income to make decisions about earning "extra" money, since they have tax payable in addition to taxes deducted at source. Each place that deducts taxes at source assumes it is the only place you earn income. A typical pensioner may earn income from CPP, Old Age Security, pensions, RRSPs, RIFs or other investment income. These people need to understand their marginal tax rate so they can use that information when planning to take additional income by cashing in RRSPs, or selling investment properties in years when their income is low.

Marginal rates could also be used to determine the amount of RRSPs you purchase. Because the purchase of RRSPs "lowers" your income, it can move you to a different marginal tax bracket. In a similar fashion, the impact of various deductions can be weighed.

Confused? Don't be. While your accountant cannot make decisions for you, he can help you sort through the repercussions of those decisions. Your main goal? No tax surprises!

🌓 KEY INSIGHT

When working with discretionary income or expenses, consider your marginal tax bracket.

NOTES:_____

_____

_____

TIP #48: KNOW THE DIFFERENCE BETWEEN A TAX CREDIT AND A TAX DEDUCTION.

Tax credits and tax deductions are not the same thing — and they are taxed differently.

A **tax deduction** is a reduction in your taxable income and the tax savings are calculated at your marginal rate. If you pay into an RRSP, for example, you get a reduction at your marginal tax rate. Using the hypothetical marginal tax rate calculated in Tip #46, this means that if you make $110,000 and you contribute $5,000 to your RRSP, your tax savings would be $2,100. If you make $50,000 and contribute $5,000 to the RRSP, your tax savings would be $1,600. In short, your contribution stays the same, but the savings are based on your marginal tax rate that we used for simplification purposes.

A non-refundable **tax credit** is a reduction in taxes of the same amount, regardless of your income level. If the tax credit rate on the RRSP in the above example was 22%, your savings would be $1,100, regardless of income.

The following deductions are examples of non-refundable tax credits:

* Personal amount
* Spousal amount
* Disability amount
* Tuition and Education amount
* Charitable donation and gifts
* Medical expenses

Knowing the difference between a tax deduction and a tax credit is important, but don't get hung up on the details, since that's what your accountant is for. Your real estate investment decisions should be governed by income and capital profit, not tax avoidance. As long as you are following a proven system and your business is making money, you can find people to help you do what you want to do to create and protect long-term wealth. Successful people do not wait until they know it all. They focus on what they do best and hire other "experts" to assist where they don't have specialized knowledge.

RED FLAG

Make sure the valuations a charity gives you for a donation or gift are accurate and not inflated. If they do not stand up to scrutiny, they will be disallowed. The Canada Revenue Agency is on top of this issue.

KEY INSIGHT

Tax credits are generally calculated at the lowest tax bracket, whereas a deduction is based on your marginal tax rate. When it comes to completing your tax forms for a given year, your accountant will likely recommend you pool your medical and charitable donations to one spouse, due to additional threshold rules which apply to these specific credits. This can be difficult for some spouses to understand, but it is done to optimize tax within the *family unit*; not to make one spouse the "beneficiary" of particular tax benefits.

NOTES:_____

_____

_____

_____

_____

_____

_____

_____

_____

TIP #49: DIVIDE TAXABLE INCOME WITH INCOME SPLITTING.

Know the traps of income splitting and avoid unexpected results!

Further on the topic of "optimizing tax within the family unit," from a family's *overall tax perspective* it is often best to pool medical and charitable donations to one spouse. Dividing taxable income between spouses is another way to optimize tax within the family unit.

Known as "income splitting," this strategy allows individual spouses to capitalize on lower rates of tax, since personal tax rates are progressive. With some minor exceptions, the lower a spouse's income, the lower the tax rate. In other words, the couple pays less tax when they both claim incomes of $40,000 compared to a couple where one claims $5,000 in income and the other spouse $75,000.

Your accountant may also look for ways to divide income between other family members as well. This must be done properly, since the strategy of income splitting can yield unexpected results.

To optimize your income-splitting opportunities, keep the following possibilities in mind (and always be aware that severe consequences are possible if implemented incorrectly or in the wrong circumstances):

- Pay reasonable wages to family members for work actually performed.
- Make low-interest-rate loans (at fixed rates determined quarterly by the CRA) to low-income family members, who in turn will make investments.
- Create a corporation and pay dividends to low-income family members who are not required to work in the business. (This does not work with children who are minors. For more on the complexities of incorporation, review Tip #14.)
- Consider splitting ownership of properties or shares/units so that, upon ultimate sale, the income is split between spouses or generations.
- Allow family members to create businesses which can earn income by servicing your properties (and likely others, too).
- Consider splitting ownership of properties so the regular income from the property is divided between family members.

- Create a family trust to own property directly or indirectly and divide income (whether rental or, for example, development/ flipping/ rent-to-own etc), or for the trust to provide business services for the properties. (Again, family trusts are tricky. See Tips #74 to #76 in Part 4.)

Managing the ties that bind

It makes intuitive sense to pool business resources and expertise with the people in your family. But discussions about optimizing tax within the family unit can be complicated, even when all of the members of that family express a sincere interest in working for the common good of family legacy and wealth. The earlier you treat the family-business relationship as a true business partnership, the better. That means addressing potential conflicts and the business's dissolution, long before it appears any problems might arise.

🅢 SOPHISTICATED INVESTOR TIP

It is wise to address the breakup of your business, even if that business is managed as a co-venture with family members. Address key elements, like property valuation, the liquidation process, the buy-out process and how tax liability will be shared.

NOTES:_____

_____

_____

_____

_____

_____

_____

_____

_____

TIP #50: PAY FAMILY MEMBERS.

Family wages must be reasonable and based on work performed.

Bringing family members into your real estate investment business is another way to keep your investment profits in the family. You can, for example, pay wages to your children for tasks such as lawn care, cleaning or helping with the painting of a property. Similarly, a spouse may be paid for his or her administrative assistance in managing or maintaining a property.

Just remember that good records are invaluable, since you will need to report wages paid and your family members will need to report income earned.

Remember, too, that all wages must be reasonable based on the work performed. If not, even deductions that are reported on time via T4 slips and T4 summaries may be disallowed. It would likely be viewed as unreasonable, for example, to pay your eight-year-old daughter $15,000 to rake the leaves during the fall.

SOPHISTICATED INVESTOR TIP

Getting your children involved in real estate investing is a good way to help them learn how to take responsibility for their future financial security. *51 Success Stories from Canadian Real Estate Investors* includes several stories of how Canadian families used their real estate investment businesses to help their children earn spending money, and to help parents and children save for post-secondary education.

NOTES:_____

_____

_____

_____

_____

_____

_____

_____

_____

TIP #51: FILE T4S AND T5S ON TIME.

As a responsible employer, you must file formal reports accurately and on time.

The Canada Revenue Agency requires business people to inform the agency of many situations where they: a) pay wages to employees, or b) pay interest to other people. This is accomplished on an annual basis by reporting wages on T4 slips and T4 summaries. When interest is involved, the dividends and interest paid by corporations are reported to the CRA via T5 slips and T5 summaries.

These forms are relatively straightforward to prepare and CRA guides are available. They describe how to complete the forms and note that these forms must be received by the CRA by February 28 of each year. Failure to file appropriately or on time may result in various penalty charges.

🔴 KEY INSIGHT

Information about the forms and their completion is readily available on the CRA Web site. Make it your business to know where you can get good information about your responsibilities as an employer.

NOTES:_____

_____

_____

_____

_____

_____

_____

_____

_____

TIP #52: FORMAL REPORTING IS ESPECIALLY IMPORTANT WHEN DEALING WITH FAMILY MEMBERS.

Late T4s and T5s for family members may attract unwelcome attention from the CRA.

When dealing with family members, the formalized reporting process helps ensure that the reported amounts are acceptable to the CRA, thus entitling you to the deductions you expect. When the forms are missed or filed late, it may look like **retroactive tax planning** is taking place.

Deductions based on retroactive planning are more likely to be denied upon audit. This interpretation of the rules underlines the wisdom of Tip #13: *Never think you're special!*

 RED FLAG

The CRA may accept late payment of withheld taxes. They may also view this as retroactive tax planning. That's why paying late is a great way to attract scrutiny! Avoid any hassles by taking some time to familiarize yourself with CRA expectations about employment.

NOTES:_____

_____

_____

_____

_____

_____

_____

_____

_____

TIP #53: CAPITAL GAIN AND INCOME ARE *NOT* THE SAME THING.

Get it right the first time! It is very expensive to incorrectly assume your investment income is a capital gain.

A capital gain is the gain that results from the **sale** of a capital asset, such as stocks, bonds, art, stamp collections and real estate. Tax is paid on 50% of a capital gain. In other words, only 50% of the gain is taxable.

> **Warning!** Many novice real estate investors assume a capital gain always results when they sell properties. Reality tells a different tale — and an inappropriate tax-filing position can trigger an expensive tax problem.

Tax is charged on the capital gain (profit) that's realized on the sale of a non-inventory asset that was bought at a lower price. If, for example, you buy an apple tree and sell apples, you are in the business of selling apples. Income from the sale of those apples would be your *regular income*. When you sell that apple tree after 10 years, the *profit* from that sale would be a capital gain and you would pay tax on half the profit, or half the capital gain.

Complications set in when the business changes. If interest in that apple tree prompted you to start selling apple trees, for example, you would be in the business of selling apple trees. The trees would be, in essence, an inventoried asset. If you only sold an apple tree every few years, the decision about whether a capital gain would apply would depend on your circumstances. That's right — there could be more than one answer!

And that's the problem. Real estate investments are complicated transactions and disputes regarding capital gains **are one of the most heavily litigated areas in the courts.** Investors may erroneously believe that they can claim a capital gain after they've held a property for a certain period of time, or because the Canada Revenue Agency did not disallow the claim on an earlier transaction. (Just because the CRA missed it the first time does not mean it won't review files when questions arise in subsequent years.)

 **KEY INSIGHT**

> Advice you get over the phone from a CRA representative does not bind the agency to any decision. For more details on the tax rules regarding capital gain, look up *CRA Interpretation Bulletin 218R.*

TIP #54: WHEN IT COMES TO CAPITAL GAINS, *INTENTION* MATTERS.

Plan ahead. You may need to prove that an investment is eligible for capital gains treatment.

It is important for real estate investors to understand how tax on capital gain applies, because the purchase and sale of property is one of the financial transactions that realizes a capital gain. Let's say you bought a property for $100,000 fifteen years ago. This is the only rental property you own, and when you now sell the property for $250,000, your profit from the property is $150,000. Your taxable capital gain would be $75,000, so the tax you pay will be based on your marginal tax bracket.

Now think back to that example of the apple tree in Tip #53 and you will start to see where this can get complicated for real estate investors. With the benefit of hindsight, the Canada Revenue Agency looks for your *intention*. Here's a look at how they might view the various transactions:

1. You buy a rental property and keep it for several years. This puts you in the business of earning rental income. When you sell the property, it's like selling your apple tree and profit from the property sale would likely be a capital gain.
2. If you buy a presale condo and sell it prior to possession, the transaction was probably in the nature of trade and therefore taxable as regular income. This gets complicated if you have an unsolicited offer you can't refuse, or need to sell your investment property due to personal circumstances such as a family member's death, divorce or loss of job.
3. You buy vacant land, subdivide it and sell it. Again, this is probably a transaction in the nature of trade and hence, regular income.
4. You purchase an apartment building, strata title or condominiumize it, and sell it. Again, it's probably a transaction in the nature of trade.
5. Those who buy fixer-uppers, fix them and sell them in a short period of time are also likely making transactions in the nature of trade.

 **Key Insight**

Practice the 10% rule.

When it comes to dealing with the CRA, honesty is the only policy. Always remember that the main difference between a below-average investor and an over-achieving investor amounts to a mere 10% increase in effort. You do need to work hard. You do not need to cheat. Stick with the following four general business rules and you'll stay on the right track.

1. Only make commitments you have every intention of fulfilling.
2. Be honest if circumstances change.
3. Be prepared to take responsibility for how those new circumstances may impact your business. (Do you owe taxes you didn't expect?)
4. Never sign a document that isn't true.

Sophisticated Investor Tip

Clarity in communication is critical and good advice does not have to be complicated.

That's why sophisticated investors shop around to find a lawyer and accountant they want to work with, trust — and understand. Indeed, complex business structures and transactions may do more harm than good when you're first starting out.

Remember: if it's your signature, you're responsible. Ignorance is no defense.

NOTES:_____

_____

_____

_____

_____

_____

_____

_____

_____

_____

TIP #55: LOOK FOR WAYS TO *PROVE* YOUR PRIMARY INTENTION.

If you want to claim a capital gain, prepare to defend your decision.

A lot of wannabe investors and market greenhorns believe that as long as you hold a property for a certain period of time, you automatically acquire a capital gain. This is not true!

In reality, the Canada Revenue Agency looks for certain parameters when deciding to allow/disallow a claim of capital gain. Keep that in mind when you're brokering a deal. Real estate investors must ask themselves these questions:

- What was my *intention* at the time of purchase? In other words, was I primarily looking to earn profits from renting the property or using the property myself (indicative of a capital gain), or was the primary intention to realize a profit on the future sale of the property (indicative of income)?
  a. Was I able to implement my plans?
  b. Was I thinking of flipping?
  c. Did I list the property prior to or shortly after possession?
- What was my knowledge of the business? A real estate agent is deemed to know more about real estate than an ordinary person.
- What does the frequency of my similar transactions say about my intentions?
- How long did I keep the property?

🌑 KEY INSIGHT

The CRA wants to prove "primary intention" — and has the benefit of hindsight. CRA agents will look to see if the taxpayer (you) intended to receive income from the investment itself, or to use the property in another business (you) operate. Here, the CRA will likely decide (you) realized a capital gain. Alternatively, situations where the investor tries to generate profits from the sale of the property itself are more indicative of an income intention.

NOTES:_____

_____

_____

TIP #56: THE CRA WILL "LOOK BEHIND THE CURTAIN" FOR A BACKUP PLAN!

The CRA can deem that you intended to sell the property if the investment didn't work out as planned.

Tip #53 informed us that disputes regarding capital gains are one of the most heavily litigated areas in Canadian courts. That's true for three reasons:

1. Taxpayers do not understand the difference between profit and income;
2. Taxpayers may need to prove *intention*; and
3. There are times when the CRA, with the benefit of hindsight, deems that a taxpayer had a "secondary intention." If the CRA can prove you had a backup plan to sell the property if the investment didn't work out the way you wanted, **the profit may be classified as income!**

Keep in mind, too, that your benefits may be less than your professional fees to fight the case.

POINTS TO CONSIDER

On the plus side for real estate investors, Canadian courts have taken into consideration a wide variety of factors to help them interpret the intentions of taxpayers. None of the following indicators is a final determinant, but investors should keep these factors in mind when calculating how the CRA may interpret a claim in favour of either capital gain or income.

- Feasibility. Can you realistically do what you say you want to do?
- Extent to which plans were carried out.
- Geography and zoning. Are you buying in a speculative area or does zoning permit your stated intentions?
- Nature of the property. Developed versus undeveloped? High-versus-low-income capacity?
- Frustration of primary intent. Did something beyond your control keep you from implementing your plans?
- Business organization. Do you look like a sophisticated business?
- Efforts made to effect sale. Unsolicited versus MLS listing? Do you have a marketing plan?

- Evidence of change of intention. Intention to convert to condo status?
- Nature of business of taxpayer/associates.
- Use of borrowed money and terms. Leverage? Open/closed? Capacity for income?
- Length of time property held. Be very cautious when dealing with rules of thumb!
- Other participants. Intentions of controlling party? Occupations of others in the deal?
- Reasons for sale which may indicate original intention.
- Evidence of extensive dealings with real estate.

 **KEY INSIGHT**

The CRA's efforts to "prove" primary and secondary intentions are loaded with subjectivity. Make your case based on credibility and integrity. Keep good records. Where possible, separate your properties between capital gain and income. Document your thoughts and plans before you complete transactions. Appreciate that legal concerns may trump tax considerations.

SOPHISTICATED INVESTOR TIP

Fine-tune your understanding of capital gains
by George Dube, CA

Preparation and education can help shield you from a tax disaster. Generally speaking, investors who personally own real estate will want to pursue a capital gain on profit, since only 50% of the profits from a capital gain are taxed. Tax rate differences between individuals and corporations may mean there will be times when a business person prefers to treat profit as income. Other strategic reasons to claim capital gain versus income include:

- Capital cost allowance is available to capital assets, but not inventory.
- Differences in the period of time you can carry a tax reserve and bring profits into income (potentially over 3 or 5 years).
- Restrictions on tax-free reorganizations (methods of transferring ownership of properties or corporate shares, for example, without immediately incurring taxes — frequently used in estate and succession planning).
- Restrictions on the deductibility of certain costs which may otherwise need to be included as a cost of the inventory and thus are not deducted until the property is sold.

TIP #57: GET TO KNOW THE CONCEPT OF CAPITAL COST ALLOWANCE.

Different assets qualify for different rates of CCA.

Capital cost allowance (CCA) can be thought of as the tax equivalent to the depreciation you are allowed to expense for accounting purposes. It applies to fixed assets, except land, for example, and different types of assets are allocated to different CCA classes. Most automobiles, for example, are Class 10 or 10.1. Class 10 and 10.1 items can be expensed at 30% per year on a declining balance basis. That said, the CCA allowed in the *first year* an asset is purchased is usually only 50% of the normal amount. That means CCA for Class 10 would be 15% in the first year.

CCA AND REAL ESTATE

The CCA rate is relatively low for buildings; often 4%, and zero for land. To capitalize on the CCA on the purchase price of a property, you need to give some extra thought to how the purchase price of your property is allocated. To do this, consider analyzing the property so you can justify an allocation of the purchase price to the building and land, as well as to items like furniture, appliances, fences, swimming pools, parking lots, roads, sidewalks, outdoor signage and sheds.

Say, for example, the purchase price of a property is $200,000. The standard process is to claim a certain amount for land, say 25% or $50,000, and the difference to the building. Consider as an alternative an allocation such as this:

Land	$35,000
Parking lot	$15,000
Fence	$3,000
Walkway	$5,000
Shed	$5,000
Appliances	$7,000
Furniture	$3,000
Building	$127,000
Total	$200,000

Where the assets are in higher rate CCA classes, you will be able to claim the CCA faster. That means you can shield more of your income faster. Although you would eventually get the same amount of deductions over a number of years regardless of the class in which you put depreciable assets (other than land), do not wait the extra time if you have income to protect from taxes.

🔴 KEY INSIGHT

Capital cost allowance (CCA) is complicated, since depreciable items are deemed to belong to different classes and those classes depreciate at different rates. How much you can claim each year also depends on when you acquired the property. For details on the classes of depreciable properties, how much CCA you can claim and "special circumstances," check out the Canada Revenue Agency's Web site, www.cra-arc.gc.ca.

🔴 SOPHISTICATED INVESTOR TIP

You don't need to be a tax expert to find value in the Canada Revenue Agency's Web site. Make it your business to familiarize yourself with what's on the site.

NOTES:_____

_____

_____

_____

_____

_____

_____

_____

_____

_____

TIP #58: MAKE CAPITAL COST ALLOWANCE WORK FOR YOU.

Ask your accountant about using the CCA as a tax-free and interest-free loan from the CRA.

Since buildings do not truly depreciate in value until later in their life, or where they receive insufficient maintenance, novice investors may wonder whether CCA is ever applicable! It's a good question, and the "right answer" is the reason why real estate investors need a business plan that incorporates tax strategy.

Tip #57 told us the Canada Revenue Agency allows us to slowly deduct the cost of a building over time (and only if there is a profit). Various exceptions and restrictions exist, but for residential buildings, the CCA rate is typically 4% per year. That means that every year we may be able to deduct 4% of the cost of the building which we haven't previously deducted.

This is where your tax strategy comes into play. In the future, if a building sells at a value greater than the cost, the CRA will include all previously claimed CCA into your income. This may seem unfair, but think about it. By claiming CCA, you were allowed to expense a portion of the building that was to represent the decrease in value over time. If, at the end of your ownership, the building has appreciated, you need to take back into your income the previously-claimed depreciation.

So, where's the advantage in claiming a deduction we have to pay back later? Since we claim the deduction and saved those taxes over the period of time we owned the building, we only have to pay taxes back when that property is sold. That's not difficult, since we now have cash available from the sale.

We have, in other words, used the government's money to operate our business. Now that we can bank the success, we can pay the government back.

Caution!

Real estate investors should **almost NEVER** claim CCA when you may be able to use the "principal residence exemption" on a property. The principal residence exemption can make the profits on the sale of a property tax-free. Claiming CCA will make the property ineligible for the claim — and cannot be changed retroactively. For more on principal residency, review Tip #15: Your home is your castle.

TIP #59: YOU *WILL BE* AUDITED.

You don't have to like the audit. You do need to plan for it.

There are three types of audits: An information request, a desk audit and a full audit.

The *information request* is as straightforward as an audit gets. Here, Canada Revenue Agency computers may scan a filed return and compare it with information from other sources, generating a request for some specific information. Other requests for information may come from manual determinations and tax-adjustment requests. Regardless of what precipitates the information request, an information request may be done as a pre-assessment shortly after filing. Alternatively, after a more significant period of time, the CRA may request further details, frequently in the fall/early winter of the same year you filed.

A *desk audit* occurs when the CRA requests that you gather information and send it to the agency. You will have a better chance if your information is clean. These requests are generally answered via letters or the telephone, so you do not have to meet with CRA personnel.

The third kind of audit is a *full audit* — and it's all about face-to-face meetings with CRA personnel. Here are some things you can do to ease the process:

1. Read the CRA request carefully and provide personnel with the data they need.
2. Be courteous. Show agency staff where they can get coffee, water and washrooms.
3. Provide them with a comfortable area to sit and work.
4. Ask them to provide written questions and respond to their queries once or twice a day.

🕐 KEY INSIGHT

An auditor may ask you to sit across the desk and answer questions as they proceed through the papers. Try to avoid this as it is not a good use of your time. This is much less likely to be a problem if your records are easy to find and easy to follow.

Remember: it's the auditor's job to ask questions. It's your job to deliver answers. You must answer those questions truthfully, too. Do not guess the answer. "I don't know," or "I don't remember," are acceptable answers.

TIP #60: AVOID UNNECESSARY CONFLICT WITH THE AUDITOR.

Use credible records to make your case.

The auditor is there to collect money in the easiest possible manner. Your objective is not to give them any more money than you are required to under law, so no wonder there's conflict!

Generally speaking, business people who have to pay more money after an audit do not have the proper documentation for their deductions. While you may get an auditor who allows certain expenses on the basis of *reasonableness*, never assume that will happen. Instead, keep your records clean and accurate and the paper trail direct.

Create a relationship, not an armed camp

Real Estate Investing in Canada walked readers through the 18 Rules of Negotiation. These are good rules to put into your system and it's a good idea to review them regularly — and long before you are ever audited. Ten of those rules are of special note to the audit process. They are:

1. Create a Relationship, Not an Armed Camp,
2. Seek a Win-Win Deal,
3. Separate People from the Problem,
4. Focus on Motivations, Not Taking Positions,
5. Search for Agreement,
6. Listen to Reason, not Pressure,
7. Do Your Homework and Know Your Options,
8. Be Patient,
9. Never Abuse; Always Amuse and
10. Follow Through.

NOTES:_____
_____
_____
_____
_____
_____

TIP #61: RECONSIDER SELF-REPRESENTATION.

You may have nothing to hide. But do you really know the rules?

You can represent yourself in an audit and most people who make that decision do so because they know they've got nothing to hide. That's fine. But this is a good time to review the first tip in this section:

Tax is not about fairness, it's about rules.

The CRA auditor has been trained to do audits. You may or may not have even prepared your own tax return!

🔑 KEY INSIGHT

In many cases, your advisor can help guide the audit process so that less of everyone's time is spent on non-productive issues and the heart of the matter can be addressed in short order.

NOTES:_____

_____

_____

_____

_____

_____

_____

_____

_____

TIP #62: RULE BREAKERS INVITE SCRUTINY.

There is more than random selection at work!

There is no simple answer as to why a particular tax return is selected for audit. Indeed, the Canada Revenue Agency often cites *random selection*. That may be true in some cases, but accounting professionals say business people can invite CRA scrutiny when they don't pay enough attention to the rules. More specifically:

1. Are your numbers in line with industry norms?
2. Do those numbers red flag the potential for abuse?
3. Automotive, entertainment and travel expenses are the most prone to abuse. Will the numbers on these line items attract the CRA's attention?

THIRD-PARTY INFORMATION

The next source of audit is third-party information. This comes to light, for example, when the CRA goes to the land titles office and notices you sold a property that is not reported on your tax return. Similar information is also available for cars from motor vehicles branches. When the CRA audits a car dealership, it may notice that one customer is buying a lot of cars. This kind of activity may make the CRA suspicious that the person is selling cars and not reporting the income.

RED FLAG

Remember that age-old adage about keeping your friends close and your enemies closer? Disgruntled employees, business associates and former spouses also call the CRA with information that may lead to an audit!

Late filers may also attract scrutiny. This is often a clue that individuals are not well organized and may not be able to track receipts. This makes them an easy target for an audit.

KEY INSIGHT

Let an accountant handle your audit. They are experienced and are not emotionally attached to the numbers.

TIP #63: STATUTES OF LIMITATIONS ON AUDITS.

Different government departments have different audit periods.

A statute of limitations limits how long after filing a tax return you can be audited. But different departments have different audit periods and objectives, so never assume you are always working with the same timelines. Some of the more common statutes of limitations are calculated from the following:

1. *Date from which a notice of assessment was mailed or the last notice of reassessment was mailed for that year.* The Canada Revenue Agency sends you a notice of assessment after you file a personal tax return and corporate return. This is mailed to you. On a personal tax return, you can be audited for three years from that date. Sometimes you or the CRA will reassess your return because you made a mistake on a return. Generally speaking, a T-slip was missed because it came late or you simply forgot it. Other times, you may miss a deduction because you forgot to hand the information to your accountant, or a deduction was missed in the accountant's office.
2. *Date the CRA received the tax return.*
3. *Date of mailing of the return.*

GST/HST IS DIFFERENT

For a GST/HST return, you generally have four years from the mailing of the last notice of assessment or reassessment. This means the CRA can audit any GST/HST returns in the previous four years. All GST/HST returns prior to that period are time-barred and cannot be audited.

PERMANENT RECORDS

Review Tip #26: You should keep permanent files. Considering all you've learned about how the CRA uses hindsight to determine your intentions, it's easy to see how credible and accessible permanent records can save you time, money and oodles of frustration.

Help! I'm Being Audited!

Fear is probably the first and most common response to news that you are going to be audited. Take a deep breath! The auditors are looking for signs of tax evasion, but if you have not engaged in tax evasion, you likely have nothing to worry about. Experienced investors know that tax audits can be part of doing business. Rather than sweat the details of tax law, including statutes of limitations, they let their tax professional guide them through the audit process.

 RED FLAG

Statutes of limitations are void in cases of fraud, misrepresentation or negligence. Fraud, misrepresentation or negligence do not carry a statute of limitations. Negligence may include poor record-keeping, resulting in incorrectly reported income or expenditures. In the authors' opinion, the broad definitions of negligence cited by the courts in recent years has practically eliminated the concept of any time limitations.

NOTES:_____
_____
_____
_____
_____
_____
_____
_____
_____

◐ INVESTOR-IN-ACTION: TONY PETERS

Good advice is essential for investment success.

Tony and Jo-Ann Peters were primed for success when they rolled out a brand-new business venture in 2007. Having done all the management, marketing and legal legwork to sell franchises to real estate investors who wanted to sell lease-to-own properties by following the proven systems that Tony and Jo-Ann had pioneered, the couple was justifiably excited about the prospect of helping *thousands* of Canadians buy their own homes.

Looking back on a business venture they've since wound down, Tony is confident they did everything they could to make the idea work. He's also sure it made sense to adapt to a new business model when the franchise model proved too complicated to pursue, especially given the fact that their own real estate investment portfolio also needed their attention. Sometimes, great ideas can also be great distractions from what is already working.

What's really important here is that Tony and Jo-Ann set their goals high, did what it took to make those goals happen, and never let anyone steal their dream. The fact they didn't hit the exact target is moot, since their own investment business is now stronger because of what they did, what they learned and what they now know about where their business is headed.

That sense of direction owes much to the legal and accounting advice they sought along the way. A variety of legal specialists helped them navigate the complicated territory associated with launching a franchise enterprise, and Tony depends on their chartered accountant to help them through the details of what Parts 5 and 6 are all about: the ins and outs of Canadian tax law.

As you read through their story, pay attention to how systems continue to play a major role in helping Tony and Jo-Ann Peters meet their targets. They've obviously learned that niche marketing opportunities demand niche systems. So, if you really want to be a creative real estate investor, you'd better be serious about creative systems, too.

* * *

Tony and Jo-Ann Peters stopped counting the number of revenue and lease-to-own properties they'd transacted soon after their portfolio passed the 250 mark. But don't get hung up on their inability to attach a specific number to their portfolio of residential properties on any given day: Tony and Jo-Ann carefully track the numbers that count. Indeed, Tony is quick to dismiss real estate investors who tell him they don't want to be bothered by the numbers side of their investment businesses.

"I've talked to people who tell me they want to buy real estate but *hate* the legal, accounting and financial management side of the business. Let me tell you, that's a side of the business you better get good at if you're serious about making money," says Tony, president of Creative Housing Solutions Inc. and a suite of related corporations with a keen focus on the lease-to-own residential real estate market.

Investing in Canadian real estate since 2001, Tony is all about the niche market and targeted the lease-to-own market from the get-go. But doing things differently, or "creatively," as Tony likes to say, doesn't mean you can't learn from the mistakes of others. Indeed, from where Tony sits, that's the only way to go.

He and Jo-Ann enrolled in their first REIN weekend program in the fall of 2001. Weeks later they were buying property, with Tony headlining the property search and acquisition and Jo-Ann handling the books. By mid-2007, they had transacted 150 revenue and lease-to-own properties, were holding 60 doors and were pushing ahead with plans to franchise Creative Housing Solutions Canada, a lease-to-own company they started in 2003.

A Canadian version of a successful U.S.-based investment strategy, Creative Housing Solutions Canada was set up to help renters buy their principal residences. By the time they decided to enter the franchise market, Tony and Jo-Ann had already helped more than 50 renters buy their own homes. They were also fielding a growing number of requests from others who wanted to emulate their success by using their approach. Or so they said.

Tony liked the idea of sharing strategies, but was concerned about quality control. As it turns out, that trepidation was well placed. Even though they spent a year on legal issues and branding and eventually sold seven franchises, Tony faced ongoing problems with franchisees who signed documents saying they would operate the business one way and then did something else their own way. Having worked with tax, copyright, trademark and intellectual property rights lawyers to set the business up, Tony knew that successful franchises couldn't afford a weak link. "The franchisees wanted to do their own thing and that was not a good thing for us," he recalls.

Not prepared to stick by a business model with more frustrations than they were willing to put up with, Tony and Jo-Ann took a tough look at the model and came up with a new approach. They still manage their own portfolio of long-term-hold and lease-to-own properties. But instead of selling (and managing) franchisees, they teach others what they do. "We went from being students to being able to share our experiences with others and it's been great!" says Tony.

Their new mission, which says they are "committed to educating, motivating and empowering others to take action," is a good fit with a corporate philosophy that builds on the age-old wisdom about living life as a journey, not a destination. That implies a willingness to learn as you go and to be prepared to change your route when a new one holds more promise. It doesn't mean blind change. "You need to seek counsel from the experts and from people who practice what they preach," says Tony.

That focus on education extends to the professionals who work with them, too. When Tony learned about family trusts, he got excited and went to his chartered accountant for help. The CA tried to talk him out of the idea, but agreed to investigate further by attending a seminar with Jo-Ann. "In the end, he only charged us for an hour of his time instead of two because he learned new information," notes Tony.

The fact that Tony was willing to pay the CA for two hours of his time sets him apart. And that's okay with Tony. He took a similar bring-in-the-pros approach to the franchise concept and has no regrets. "You can't be afraid to spend a little money in those areas because quality information is a wise investment."

Further to that, his top advice to new and experienced real estate investors warns against free information. "People gravitate towards free information, but why?" asks Tony. "The people with free information are the least qualified and they're the most eager to provide information because they don't have to take any responsibility for being wrong." Besides that, "free" information and seminars often lead to a sales pitch, so they are really not free.

* * *

ACTION STEPS

✓ Where can you go to learn more information about Canadian tax law as it relates to real estate investing?
✓ Are there seminars you could invite your tax lawyer and accountant to attend with you?

✓ Have you shared information you have learned with the professional members of your real estate investment team?

✓ Are your business goals "big enough"? Good ideas for niche market investments take time to develop. What can you do to make sure you are thinking big — and taking action?

PART 6

LET'S GET SOPHISTICATED: TAX STRATEGIES FOR THE SAVVY INVESTOR.

TIP #64: MONITOR YOUR CAPITAL DIVIDEND ACCOUNT.

A capital dividend account is one way to extract cash from a corporation on a tax-free basis.

With a capital dividend account, qualifying corporations can pay out the tax-free portion of a capital gain to the shareholders, who do not incur any personal tax.

How does this work? Say a company sells a property for $300,000. It originally paid $140,000 for the property, so a $160,000 capital gain results. Half of this $160,000 would be taxed, with the other half earned by the company tax-free. To put the shareholders of a company on a comparative basis with an individual who earns the same capital gain and is able to keep $80,000 tax-free, the Canada Revenue Agency allows shareholders to extract this same $80,000 from the company via a capital dividend account.

To receive this cash tax-free, some tax and legal documentation must be completed prior to paying out the dividend. The paperwork must also be submitted to the CRA prior to payment of the dividend. One of the primary requirements in completing the documentation is that a schedule must be prepared outlining the tax-free amount that can be withdrawn. This can be straightforward, but since the calculation is done on a cumulative basis from the creation of the company, it may prove a little more daunting.

Moreover, failure to follow the correct rules can result in significant penalties and unintended results.

🌑 KEY INSIGHT

The basic rules regarding a capital dividend account are not overly complex. But it is easy to make mistakes and errors can be costly. Again, professional assistance is highly recommended.

NOTES:_____

_____

_____

_____

_____

Tip #65: There may be tax implications to refinancing a property.

Tax planning cannot be retroactive, so get advice before you make decisions.

When you refinance a property you own personally, the interest you paid on the loan may or may not be deductible. It depends on what you used the funds for. If they were used for personal use, the interest is not deductible. On the other hand, if you used the money for qualified investment purposes, the interest will be deductible. The funds received on refinancing will not, however, be taxable.

In a corporation, these mechanics change. Here, if you take funds out of a corporation, they may be taxable regardless of how you use them. Here is an example of how this works, using a property purchased at $1 million as an example.

- Purchase price: $1 million
- A partner pays a down payment of $200,000, plus an extra $50,000 for renovations
- The original mortgage amount: $800,000
- Your investment: $ 0

Once renovations are complete, you have the property appraised and your numbers look like this

- Property value $ 1.5 million
- New mortgage $ 1.2 million
- Pay out old mortgage $800,000
- Cash left: $400,000

Let's say at this point you meet with your partner and decide you will pay back your partner's original investment of $250,000, with the balance of $150,000 split between you ($75,000 to each). The original $250,000 being paid to the partner is not an issue. It is paid back on a tax-free basis as that was his original shareholder's loan. The $75,000 becomes a dividend to each of you. Normally, you would pay tax on this amount.

You may be able to get some corporate taxes refunded as a result of paying these dividends, but talk to your accountant first. It is much easier to make adjustments to business decisions before a transaction takes place, and investors who wait until they see their tax bill will be disappointed to learn that you can't undo the tax implications of certain business choices.

This is why sophisticated investors make tax decisions on the advice of their tax professionals. Still determined to go it alone? The Income Tax Act is more than 1,500 pages long, and the applications of its rules are complicated.

🌑 KEY INSIGHT

You cannot plan your tax strategy retroactively, so always make sure your tax professional knows what you plan to do. Strategic advice is the best way to avoid problems.

NOTES:_____

_____

_____

_____

_____

_____

_____

_____

_____

_____

TIP #66: USE **RDTOH** TO CUT CORPORATE TAXES.

RDTOH can cut a significant tax burden.

Although there are some exceptions, rental income is typically considered "inactive" income and applicable corporate tax rates can be high. Using Ontario as an example, the initial corporate tax rate in 2012 is 46.41% (compared to the maximum 2012 personal Ontario rate of 46.41%). At first glance, this looks ominous for investors!

It is possible, however, to pay out dividends from the company and receive the Refundable Dividend Tax On Hand (RDTOH), which translates into a refund of 26.67% — an amount that's roughly half the corporate tax burden. That's right. Instead of paying corporate taxes of 46.41%, the net tax may be 19.75%, provided various rules are followed and the company is eligible for the refund.

WHAT DO YOU NEED TO KNOW?

In paying the dividends, personal taxes will result to the shareholder. That leads to the question: How much in taxes will the recipient pay?

The majority of dividends paid to Canadian residents are taxed in a very favourable manner as compared to other sources of income. It is possible in 2012, for instance, to pay approximately $38,000 of dividends to a resident of Ontario without triggering any personal taxes (other than the $450 Ontario Health Premium) due to the "dividend tax credit." This strategy can be particularly attractive where several shareholders with otherwise low levels of income can earn the dividends.

Do note that other prohibitive taxes prevent minor children from receiving the income at a tax-favourable rate. As personal income levels increase, the benefits also decrease, potentially creating a slight tax disadvantage unless carefully planned.

 **KEY INSIGHT**

Properly structured, it is possible to turn an otherwise significant tax burden into roughly half the problem by using the RDTOH. Further, there are a variety of techniques which will enhance these benefits in many cases.

TIP #67: YOU CAN TRANSFER PERSONALLY OWNED REAL ESTATE TO A CORPORATION THROUGH A "ROLLOVER."

Learn the pros and cons to rollovers.

When you transfer personally owned real estate to a corporation, the Canada Revenue Agency will typically tax you on the accrued gain in the property as if you sold the property at fair market value to an arm's-length individual. While it may be possible to complete a tax rollover that bypasses the gain at the time of transfer, the issue is complicated and you will need professional help to weigh the advantages and disadvantages of transferring property.

Some of the pros and cons of transferring property to consider include:

Pros
• Allows deferral of tax on accrued gains
• Removes property from personal hands, which may provide advantages in financing future properties and the ability to create future wealth
• Possible estate-planning advantages
• Possible legal advantages to holding property through a corporation
• Tax advantages may be realized, although some disadvantages may also arise.

Cons
• Not all property is eligible for transfer (for example, property that is considered inventory or where non-residents are involved)
• Land-transfer tax will be charged where applicable
• Legal and accounting fees will be required to complete transfer
• Mortgage holder's fees to transfer (including their lawyer's) where applicable.

NOTES:_____
_____
_____
_____
_____

TIP #68: THERE ARE BETTER WAYS TO TRANSFER PROPERTY TO A FAMILY MEMBER.

Gifted assets are better than a discounted sale, which will leave you and the family member with a capital gain.

At first glance, it may look like a good idea to sell your child a rental property while giving them a break on the price. In reality, this kind of sale spells tax disaster!

Say you want to sell to your child for $60,000 a property worth $100,000. Perhaps you acquired this property years ago for $25,000. Ignoring any potential taxes generated on "recapture" (income included as a result of previously claimed capital cost allowance / depreciation) you will have to pay taxes on a $75,000 capital gain. Your child, however, receives the property with a cost base of $60,000. If she eventually sells the property for $130,000, she would face the taxes payable on a capital gain of $70,000.

Instead of the discounted sale, consider selling the property for $100,000. Your child can provide cash of $60,000 and acquire a note, or loan, for the remaining $40,000. You can subsequently gift your child the $40,000, meaning you effectively pay that amount yourself.

With this scenario, you still have the taxes on the capital gain of $75,000, but at least your child will have a full $100,000 cost base.

 **KEY INSIGHT**

It is almost always better to gift assets, or sell them at fair market value.

NOTES:_____

_____

_____

_____

_____

_____

_____

_____

_____

TIP #69: SPOUSAL TRANSFER OF OWNERSHIP PERCENTAGES CAN TRIGGER OTHER TAXES.

Switching ownership percentages to change who claims the income or loss is not a legitimate way to adjust income.

In Tip #16, we learned the long-term implications of whose name goes on a title. In Tip #48, we looked at why your tax professional may advise you to pool medical and charitable donations to one spouse, and in Tip #49 we saw how income splitting between spouses can lower tax. All of these tips underline the basic need to ensure business decisions are made with tax issues in mind.

Ownership percentages are a similar issue in that your tax advisor should be looking at both spouses' information. In an attempt to save taxes, spouses may try to adjust their *ownership percentage* to help shift income to the lower-income spouse, or losses to the spouse with the higher income. In other words, a wife may own 80% of a property, with the remainder owned by the husband. In subsequent years, this percentage could be evened out to 50/50, or be changed to 100/0.

Significant savings can result when income is appropriately allocated between spouses. But improperly switching ownership in a property in order to adjust who claims the income or loss from a property is not a legitimate way to accomplish this. Indeed, it carries other consequences.

When ownership changes normally, a disposition of an asset occurs, thus triggering a taxable event. This may generate a gain or loss. The sale can also create unintended taxes. In related-party situations, for example, gains are taxed and losses will often be denied.

While spousal transfers can be arranged such that there are no capital gains, "attribution" may still result. The attribution rules can allow the CRA to redirect income that nominally is earned by one spouse and transfer it back to the spouse who originally owned the asset which is generating the income. Thus, even though the property is transferred to a spouse, say the husband, the income would remain with the wife, as she originally owned the property.

NOTES:_____

_____

_____

_____

TIP #70: KNOW WHAT TRIGGERS THE ATTRIBUTION RULES WITH REAL ESTATE.

These rules present a kind of hidden time bomb for real estate investors!

Transfer of percentage of ownership is one way to trigger the Canada Revenue Agency's attribution rules. Sophisticated investors recognize these rules as one of the CRA's hidden time bombs, since an offside strategy may not be disallowed (and penalized!) for several years. Once a strategy is disallowed, significant income will be attributed back to the high-income earner. This triggers a high rate of tax, penalties and non-deductible interest, all of which can be financially devastating.

HERE'S WHAT YOU NEED TO KNOW

Generally speaking, the CRA wants to avoid scenarios where high-income individuals transfer assets to family members who then use those assets to generate income or capital gains. In the CRA's eyes, this income should have been earned by the high-income individual, and thus be taxed at a higher tax rate.

Let's consider a typical scenario where the attribution rules can be triggered. Say one spouse earns minimal income, whereas the other is the family's primary income earner. The couple decides to personally acquire a property and split the ownership along with related income/losses on an equal basis. It will be very difficult for the lower-income spouse to demonstrate where the source of cash came from to acquire his or her portion of the property. In effect, the higher-income spouse's wages were used as the funding vehicle for the deposit and initial cash resources. Since the higher-income spouse effectively acquired the property with his or her assets, the income/losses from the property should go to that individual. Failure to do this could result in application of the attribution rules. Another common scenario that triggers the attribution rules occurs when parents place a property in the name of a minor child.

What investors need to understand is that it is possible for the income of a property to be attributed and, in the case of spouses, the capital gains/losses may also be attributed. Interestingly enough, however, savvy investors know capital gains from minors or adult children are not subject to the attribution rules.

The bottom line is that the attribution rules are complex, since there is a web of rules to watch for. That said, there are also legitimate ways to effectively accomplish many of the same goals the attribution rules are partially designed to prevent.

Keep sight of your business goal

The masses may think it's bad to pay taxes, but sophisticated real estate investors know you pay a lot of tax when you make a lot of money. A proactive business plan will help you look for tax-advantaged ways to operate your business. Work with your tax professional to decide your best strategies. Steer clear of business decisions that value tax avoidance over income and profit, but make it your business to have strategies in place where you pay the least amount of tax legally allowed.

🔑 KEY INSIGHT

The attribution rules are tricky — and can be costly. Work with your accountant to structure your family's financial affairs such that you can deal with the rules in advance of your purchases and with a view to the long term. But do be careful. The CRA can also use another portion of legislation, the *General Anti Avoidance Rule*, to thwart some other tax strategies.

NOTES:_____

_____

_____

_____

_____

_____

_____

_____

_____

TIP #71: OFFER THE VENDOR A TAX DEFERRAL IF THE VENDOR TAKES BACK A MORTGAGE.

You can help defer the taxes on a portion of the capital gains if the vendor accepts a vendor take back mortgage.

A vendor take back (VTB) mortgage can be a good way to finance a real estate investment. There may also be tax benefits to the vendor, who can defer a portion of the taxable portion of the capital gains if he takes a VTB mortgage. The vendor can, for instance, elect to defer the taxes on the ratio of the portion of monies collected to the total capital gains over a maximum of five years. (This does not apply to a vendor's principal residence, as the vendor does not pay taxes on the principal residence.)

Here's a look at how a vendor can defer a portion of taxes if he accepts a VTB:

Say you buy a property for $100,000 and it is not your principal residence, so you must pay tax on the capital gains when you sell it. If you sell the property for $250,000 and take back a mortgage of $150,000 repayable in 10 annual payments of $15,000 each, then you can defer a portion of the capital gain.

Cost: $ 100,000
Selling price: $ 250,000
Capital gain: $ 150,000
Initial proceeds: $ 100,000
Vendor Take Back: $ 150,000
1/5 of capital gain: $ 30,000
Annual payment: $ 15,000

The amount of capital gains you can defer and have to take into income in each of the next five years is as follows:

In the year you sell, you can defer $90,000.
Deferral = the lesser of:
(Proceeds not due until after the year/Total proceeds) X capital gains
($150,000 / $ 250,000) X $150,000 = $90,000
Or:
$150,000 (capital gain) × 80% = $120,000

That year, you have to report a capital gain of $60,000, which equals the normal gain of $150,000 less the maximum reserve of $90,000.

In Year 2, the vendor has to report $9,000
($90,000 Balance to report - $81,000)

The deferral in Year 2 and subsequent years shall be the lower of:
(Proceeds not due until after the year/ Total Proceeds) × Capital Gain = Deferral
($135,000/ $250,000) × $150,000 = $81,000
Or:
$150,000 (Capital Gain) × 60% = $90,000

In carrying through the calculations in Year 3, the vendor has to report $21,000 while in each of Year 4 and Year 5, the vendor has to report $30,000.

NOTES:_____
_____
_____
_____
_____
_____
_____
_____
_____

TIP # 72: FIGURE OUT HOW TO MAKE THE MORTGAGE ON YOUR HOME TAX DEDUCTIBLE.

A non-deductible interest expense can be fully deductible over time!

You can make the mortgage on your home tax deductible. Sometimes called the Smith Manoeuvre (named after Fraser Smith, who brilliantly described ways to convert otherwise non-deductible interest expense into fully deductible interest costs over a period of time), the strategy actually takes several forms. Indeed, various versions of the plan exist and several have earned the support of court decisions, including a recent one from the Supreme Court of Canada rendered in January 2009.

In the basic version of a typical plan, you may have, for example, a house with a value of $200,000. Say the outstanding mortgage on the residence is $120,000. In many situations, it will be relatively easy for you to obtain a mortgage of at least $150,000 on this property (75% loan to value). You could also obtain a mortgage product from various institutions which allows you to effectively place a mortgage and /or line of credit on the property for $150,000. That would be tracked in at least two segments. In one segment, the bad/non-deductible mortgage would equal $120,000. The good/investment line of credit would be available for the difference between $150,000 and the outstanding "bad" debt, initially $30,000 in this example. As you make payments on the "bad" debt, the amount you have available to borrow and invest with increases — although the total is never more than $150,000.

This means you could invest in real estate, mutual funds, your corporation or other qualified investments and receive a tax deduction for the interest related to the "good" debt. These tax deductions then provide you with more cash flow, which in turn can be used to pay off more "bad" debt and increase the "good" debt. The more that can be paid down of the bad debt, the sooner you are deducting all of your interest costs. Keep in mind that in this scenario, you do not pay off the debt. In theory, you certainly could. But most real estate investors are happy to accept additional cheap financing that is fully tax deductible.

The strategy and related ones are certainly not for everyone, as there are pros and cons. As with all long-term strategies for wealth and tax management, however, the majority of real estate investors should discuss the possibilities with their advisors to see whether such a plan would make sense in *your* case.

Tip #73: Different GST/HST rules may apply.

GST/HST rules for investors are complicated, so don't assume, ask.

Landlords renting residential units do not generally have to actively deal with the GST/HST. That changes when you rent to businesses (non-residential) since, regardless of the nature of the property, you must charge GST/HST on the rent if you are over the registration threshold of $30,000 on a combined basis, or if you voluntarily register for GST/HST.

 RED FLAG

The CRA could deduct GST/HST from your portion of the rental income!

Failure to charge GST/HST on non-residential property ultimately means the Canada Revenue Agency will take the GST/HST out of your portion of the rent. If you charge $1,000 per month to rent a unit to a business and failed to charge GST/HST, the CRA will ask you for the GST/HST. Based on the current GST of 5%, and assuming HST is not applicable, you could have to pay the CRA $50 for the month. Alternatively, if the rent includes GST, your revenue drops to $952.38 ($1,000/1.05) with GST of $47.62 owing to the CRA. Either way, you're out of pocket because you forgot to charge GST. If you live in a province with a harmonized tax, the taxes will be much higher.

Sophisticated investors realize that where you must charge GST/HST, you are entitled to the input tax credits related to the costs you pay. This means you can receive a refund (in practice netted against the amount of tax you pay) for the GST/HST that you must pay on items such as repairs and utilities for your property. Since there is no GST/HST required on mortgage payments, you will not get any money back for your biggest cash expenditure. Still, something is better than nothing — and experienced real estate investors do capitalize on this flow-through tax.

If you have a mix of properties where you do and don't charge GST/HST, you will need to come to a reasonable allocation of the expenses on which you are entitled a GST/HST refund. In essence, the CRA will only refund GST/HST for those expenses related to revenues which in turn generate GST/HST income for the CRA. If you are able to segregate the expenses per property (or unit, in the case of mixed-use properties), these calculations will be easier — and less open to dispute.

Generally speaking, a reasonable allocation may be based on square footage, rental revenues or the number of units. If you received $1,000 of commercial revenue and $9,000 of residential revenue, for example, you could claim the GST/HST refund on 10% of eligible costs.

> **Caution!**
> There are instances where GST/HST may need to be charged on rent beyond what is described here. These may include short-term residential rentals. As always, seek good advice!

NEW RESIDENTIAL RENTAL REBATE

Initially, the GST/HST New Housing Rebate was only available to individuals who bought a new house or condo for use as their primary residence (or that of a close relation), right after closing. This was a significant point of contention for real estate investors, since it meant investors had to pay the "lost" rebate as part of the closing adjustment with their builder. That changed in 2000, when the GST New Residential Rental Property Rebate was introduced and the numbers for this rebate now mirror those of the owner-occupier rebate.

Investors who want to take advantage of the GST/HST New Residential Rental Property Rebate will find the rules differ depending on the situation. The bottom line is that this GST/HST rebate is not limited to first-time buyers, but not everyone qualifies for it either! While you would rather not have to pay the GST/HST in these cases (directly, or indirectly you are), you should at least ensure that you get everything back that you can.

Ignoring provincial harmonization amounts, you may get up to approximately one-third of the GST refunded. Where the GST/HST rebate is collected on your behalf by a developer, for example, do ensure you receive full credit for this GST/HST. The authors have come across several situations where developers collected these funds after having purchasers sign a blizzard of documents they didn't understand. Other times, they "forget" to count the rebate, or similar rebates, as a partial payment for the property. Admittedly, the majority of developers properly administer the program and are aware of the rules, but it is your money, so watch it!

The bottom line is that, when combined with various provincial harmonization amounts, provincial sales tax rebates (transitional and permanent), federal transitional amounts (from changes to the GST rates to the timing of different provinces harmonizing their sales taxes), and transitional rules and normal rules, the rebates vary considerably. You will need to determine the latest rates applicable for you depending on your exact situation. Ontario and British Columbia, for example, implemented new rules on July 1, 2010. British Columbia will have a further set of rules in place as they return to a provincial sales tax as compared to the harmonized sales tax. Changes are to begin effective April 1, 2013 based on draft legislation available at the time of writing this book.

In terms of the new rebate, investors must also remember the following:

1. The unit bought by the investor must be a "self-contained residence" with private kitchen facilities, private bath and private living area.
2. The first tenant is "reasonably expected" to occupy the unit as their primary place of residence for at least one year.

🔑 KEY INSIGHT

It's always better to be safe than sorry! Sophisticated investors who want to take advantage of this GST/HST rebate will insist on a written lease with a minimum one-year term. Month-to-month arrangements may cost you the rebate.

3. Construction, substantial renovation or conversion of the building involved must have started after February 27, 2000. (That's when the new rebate came into effect.)
4. If investors in new homes/condos sell the property during the first full calendar year after closing, unless the purchaser requires it for use as their primary residence, the investor must repay the rebate. This means there are two separate one-year qualification rules for the GST/HST investor rebate. First, own the property for a year and second, rent it for a year.

APPLICATION GUIDELINES

Investors have two years from the end of the month in which the tax became payable (often the closing date for purchases, but a variety of other dates may apply where you are having the property built or doing it yourself) to apply for this GST/HST investor rebate. You will need to file a prescribed form (GST 524 in many cases).

TIP #74: UNDERSTAND HOW A FAMILY TRUST IS TAXED.

There are tax advantages if you create a family trust properly, so get the help of a lawyer, an accountant and maybe an appraiser.

Like incorporation (Tip #17), decisions about whether to create a family trust are often shrouded in assumptions about what's "best." What's really best is good advice based on your own situation! When you're new to investing, it's good to gather some basic facts. Here are a few of the points you'll want to keep in mind when deciding if a family trust works for you:

- A family trust is generally taxed at the *highest* rate of tax unless it allocates income to a taxable beneficiary.
- Beneficiaries are generally family members and potentially an investment corporation. When dividends from an active corporation are paid to a family trust, the full amount of the dividend is often allocated between beneficiaries so the family trust does not have taxable income.

🕐 KEY INSIGHT

A family trust is not a Do-It-Yourself project! You will need the help of a lawyer, accountant and perhaps an appraiser. You also need an accountant to coordinate the trust and determine the tax consequences of its creation.

NOTES:_____

_____

_____

_____

_____

_____

_____

_____

_____

_____

TIP #75: THERE ARE THREE PRIMARY REASONS TO CREATE A FAMILY TRUST.

Family trusts are part of long-term tax strategy.

Family trusts are complicated, but the results are often worthwhile. If you sell the shares of a qualified small business which is owned by a family trust, for example, each individual may be entitled to $750,000 of capital gains on a tax-free basis. If there are four members in your family, you could multiply the deduction, thus shielding a larger capital gain.

As noted in Tip #74, however, a family trust is taxed essentially at the highest rate of tax unless it allocates income to a taxable beneficiary. Beneficiaries are usually family members and possibly an investment corporation. While there may be no tax on any dividends paid to the investment corporation, individual beneficiaries are considered taxable. Each individual over the age of 18 with approximately $35,000 in dividend income (amounts vary per province and territory) will get that money on a tax-free basis assuming that they have no other income. Any additional income will be taxed at the person's marginal tax rates subject to the dividend tax credit.

Here are three reasons you might create a family trust:

1. **To protect assets/provide creditor proofing.**
   The trust is not perfect, but provides some assistance in this area. It is important to discuss the implications with your lawyer, as there are many exceptions.
2. **To split income or capital gains.**
   Again, a family trust could be one aspect of a long-term business, wealth accumulation, family planning and tax strategy.
3. **To provide some control over assets for a period of time.**
   This aspect of a family trust is most often associated with estate planning, education planning (see Tip #76) or protecting someone who cannot protect him or herself (like an aging adult, a minor, or someone incapacitated by a disability).

NOTES:_____

_____

_____

TIP #76: A FAMILY TRUST LETS MINORS BENEFIT FROM THE OWNERSHIP OF ASSETS THEY WOULD NOT OTHERWISE BE ALLOWED TO OWN BECAUSE OF THEIR AGES.

Funds can cover education costs, a wedding, a car and much more.

Properly created, a discretionary family trust would allow the trustees to distribute assets to the beneficiaries using guidelines established by the creator or settler of the trust. From a tax perspective, the trust provides a poor method of distributing income to minors since the "kiddie tax" effectively taxes minors at the maximum tax brackets. That said, it may be a valuable strategy in cases where you want to provide financial assistance to a young child, grandchild, niece, nephew, or others.

For the sake of demonstration, let's say you buy a property today that's 100% leveraged. By the time young children complete post-secondary schooling, they could own a property and sell or refinance it. If a family trust is in place, capital gains could be distributed at normal tax rates and income distributed after the age of majority is reached. As the children enter or complete post-secondary education (this must be recent), their income levels and personal tax brackets are likely quite low. With a trust, it is possible to give these young adults income that will be taxed in their low-rate hands, instead of providing them the leftover funds of the parents after the tax authorities have drained their share from the savings. In terms of higher education, it is quite difficult to find a more tax effective way to pay for schooling!

Funds may also be used to cover a myriad of other costs. The money can help pay for a wedding, a vehicle, a birthday party, a vacation, or even to start a savings account.

NOTES:_____

_____

_____

_____

_____

_____

TIP #77: THERE ARE FOREIGN AND DOMESTIC TAX IMPLICATIONS TO BUYING FOREIGN REAL ESTATE.

Generally speaking, Canadians are taxed on their "world-wide income."

Those new to the real estate market are often surprised to learn that a foreign real estate acquisition will trigger taxes and filing requirements both in the foreign country and at home.

Residents of Canada are generally taxed on their "world-wide income." This means that income generated is subject to Canadian income taxes even if it is also taxed in a foreign state. Further to that, various disclosure rules exist which allow the Canada Revenue Agency to learn more about your foreign assets. Failure to complete the disclosure requirements can trigger significant penalties and in recent years the CRA has started to enforce these rules more vigorously.

Some tax treaties with foreign countries may define, for example, whether capital gains are taxed in Canada. Applicable tax withholding rates may also be part of these treaties and the treaties can be examined for any special considerations.

It is also possible that you may qualify for foreign tax credits in Canada for the taxes paid to foreign tax authorities. This may help reduce (or in theory, eliminate) any "double taxation" that might result from two countries taxing the identical income.

🌑 KEY INSIGHT

The CRA is interested in expanding its tax base and the types of foreign income subject to Canadian taxes, by changing the way it defines how the income is calculated, and the instances where these taxes are applicable. These rules have been under significant analysis in the past few years. Draft legislation and recent budget items, even if they haven't been adopted, also show the ground is shifting in this area. Avoid potential problems and get qualified advice to steer you through what could be a minefield of tax implications.

NOTES:_____

_____

_____

TIP #78: IF YOU PLAN TO LEAVE CANADA, BECOME A NON-RESIDENT FOR TAX PURPOSES.

Residency impacts your tax situation.

If you plan to leave Canada to take up permanent residency in a country with a lower tax regime, talk to your tax professional and make sure you understand the rules. Among other things, you may want to stay away from Canada for two years, sell your principal residence (or lease it for at least one year without a right to cancel without cause), sell your cars, boats and other large items, give up your Canadian driver's license and provincial medical plan and show you are living in the other country via primary bank accounts, social club memberships and health plans. There are many factors which influence whether the CRA believes you are a non-resident, so be sure to consult your accountant.

Also talk to your accountant about how you can apply for a deemed disposition of your principal residence and claim a tax-free capital gain. RRSPs and pensions are also specifically excluded from the calculation of what is "real property situated in Canada."

If you are not a resident of Canada, you can cash in your RRSP by paying the withholding tax only (between 15% and 25%). But watch out for the taxes in your new tax jurisdiction.

RED FLAG

Find out all you can about the tax rates in the country you want to move to.

NOTES:_____

_____

_____

_____

_____

_____

_____

_____

_____

_____

TIP #79: NON-RESIDENT INVESTORS NEED HELP WITH NON-RESIDENT RULES.

Whether buying or selling, non-residents face different rules.

When a non-resident buys a property with an intention to rent, he or she does not have to fill out any forms. Still, it is a good idea to call an accountant — and fast! Non-residents should:

• Obtain a tax ID from the Canada Revenue Agency.
• Appoint a Canadian agent (usually the Canadian managing the non-resident's property).

As required by the CRA, the agent will be responsible for withholding 25% of the gross sales proceeds (rental income) and for filing tax returns before June 30 if the agent and non-resident file a NR6 joint election. This also allows the agent to reduce the tax withheld from 25% of gross rent to 25% of net rental income (subject to some adjustments).

SELLING IS EVEN MORE COMPLICATED

The rules for non-residents get more complicated when property is sold. Again, 25% of the selling price in the case of personal-use real estate is withheld. For rental real estate, the withholding tax is 25% of the selling price of the land and up to 50% of the selling price of the building. The agent, being the lawyer who handles this transaction for the purchaser, is responsible to ensure the taxes are paid.

A clearance certificate will reduce the withholding taxes. These are issued by the CRA and can take several months to acquire! There is a requirement to file these forms within a certain number of days. Failure to do so will attract penalties.

 **KEY INSIGHT**

Once a non-resident takes his money out of the country, tax debts are difficult to collect. This is why withholdings are a standard international practice for foreign investors.

NOTES:_____

TIP #80: RRSP MORTGAGES CAN BE A GOOD WAY TO INVEST IN REAL ESTATE.

Real estate investing can increase your net cash flow over a long period of time.

If you understand investing in real estate and have RRSPs in your portfolio, consider higher-interest-rate first and second mortgages. The process is very simple. Find a bank that allows you to open a self-administered RRSP and is willing to act as a trustee for you to hand out second mortgages. Some banks have rules about the minimum loan to value ratio, the maximum interest rates, minimum annual payments and more.

For the purposes of income tax, you will have to follow a separate set of more rigorous and limiting rules if the person you are lending to is related to you. Generally speaking, a person related to you is your spouse, father, mother, brother and sister. For the purposes of income tax, however, your brother-in-law is considered a brother, a sister-in-law is considered a sister, and so on.

Be forewarned: other nuances also exist to define to whom you are related.

Once you've opened a self-administered RRSP and determined who you are lending money to, the next step is to transfer the funds to that financial institution.

🔘 KEY INSIGHT

RRSP mortgages should be understood as financial transactions backed by real estate security. If you use your RRSP to invest this way, develop an exit strategy. You need to know three things:

1. How will you get your money if the borrower stops making payments?
2. Can you sell your mortgage to another party if you need cash?
3. What happens when the term on the mortgage expires? Is there an instant renewal or are you paid off?

DO YOUR DUE DILIGENCE

Remember the higher-interest-rate earnings come with a slightly higher risk. So do be cautious about appraisals, as they may be inflated. Also remember to do your due diligence on the person to whom you are lending money.

As the banker loaning out money, you should also ask for security similar to what a bank would request. Go through your own appraisal, building inspection and environmental reports with care. Make sure the borrower has sufficient insurance, too.

The most important thing to remember here is that an RRSP mortgage is a complex investment strategy and there can be major tax implications if it's not done correctly. Keeping that in mind, you never want to let this process be undertaken by someone who lacks significant experience in the area. Talk to people who know what they're doing and check out the "RRSP in Real Estate" section at www.realestateinvestingincanada.com.

Caution!
You may also want to consider a mortgage to yourself or relatives. This mortgage has to be CMHC insured (or a similar provider of insurance). That means the trustee will dictate the terms and conditions of this mortgage, as well as specify the insurance rate, the loan-to-value ratio, and amortization — and your income verification will be critical. Since you have to qualify for the mortgage as if you applied for a new mortgage, these are not very popular mortgage investments.

**KEY INSIGHT**

The foreclosure process is expensive, so cover your assets with due diligence! Since your long-term interest is to make interest income, you do **not** want to own the property.

SOPHISTICATED INVESTOR TIP

If you want to invest your RRSPs in mortgages, remember you must understand the rules before you break them! Failure to do this may lead the Canada Revenue Agency to deem that you have deregistered your RRSP. That is the same as if you have just cashed in your RRSP and all taxes are payable by you or your spouse (if it was a spousal RRSP).

STUDY **RRSP** STRATEGIES

To learn more about RRSP strategies and the opportunities they hold for both parties, click on the "RRSP Strategies" link at www.realestateinvesting-incanada. This complete program was written by Canada's own Mr. RRSP, Valden Palm. His story is also published in *51 Success Stories from Canadian Real Estate Investors*. (A version of that story also forms the Investor-in-Action profile that ends Part 1 of this book.)

In addition to meeting rules about not lending RRSP money to direct relatives, the investment must be commercially reasonable to make it a qualified investment in your RRSP. Commercially reasonable means that if the RRSP mortgage loan is audited by the CRA, the CRA is going to look at all aspects of the mortgage to see that it fits within the market guidelines. This requires a certified appraisal of the property to establish its value and assess whether it is commercially viable. Make sure you have that appraisal on file.

Also remember to keep a good paper trail. You will need paperwork that justifies the loan. In addition to the certified appraisal, the CRA will look for some comparisons of interest rates and some comment on why the loan-to-value ratio is higher or lower than what is normally given commercially.

More detail on RRSP mortgages is also the foundation of "RRSP Mortgages Demand Extra Attention to Detail" and "Investors Drive RRSP Mortgages." These are bonus tips in *97 Tips for Real Estate Investors* and they walk you through what you need to do to set up an RRSP mortgage.

NOTES:_____

_____

_____

_____

_____

_____

_____

_____

_____

TIP #81: THERE IS NO SUBSTITUTE FOR PREPARATION.

Real estate investment demands a number of skills — and every one of them can be learned.

If real estate investment is new to you, or you want to review the fundamentals and fine-tune your strategies for greater success, consider reading (or re-reading) books like *Real Estate Investing in Canada, 97 Tips for Canadian Real Estate Investors*, and *51 Success Stories from Canadian Real Estate Investors*.

Building on information outlined in these and other books, your #1 goal is to surround yourself with people who are successfully doing what you want to do, or want to do better. You may also want to join an organization like the Real Estate Investment Network (REIN), where others can help you learn how to use the economic fundamentals of real estate investing to take action.

Good luck!

Don R. Campbell's ACRE System Home-Study Program
The Authentic Canadian Real Estate (ACRE) System is taught in great detail through a 15-CD home-study program, *The Real Estate Investment ACRES Program*. This 100%-Canadian program details the fundamentals of real estate investment, as well as latest strategies and economic updates that include information about the top Canadian towns to invest in.

A must-have for veteran and rookie investors alike, the home-study program includes a 100% money-back guarantee. For more information about the program and how to make it yours, visit www.realestateinvestingincanada.com and click on the ACRES Program button. You can also call Don's office at 1-888-824-7346 and the folks at REIN Canada will rush the program to you.

NOTES:_____
_____
_____
_____

◣ INVESTOR-IN-ACTION: DAN HEON

The buck stops with you.

Dan Heon's real estate investment story teaches a lot of important lessons. If you've read through this book from front to back, including the Investor-in-Action profiles, as you read Dan's profile you'll realize that he has considered and applied every tip covered in the book, which is the hallmark of sophisticated investors. More importantly, you will also realize that all of the Investor-in-Action profiles are really stories about individual investors taking *personal responsibility* for the financial health and security of their real estate investment portfolios.

Dan's story is important because it shows the value of staying the course. He nearly lost his business because he wasn't paying close enough attention to his financial situation, but he recovered by taking action. He hired quality bookkeeping and accounting services and became a true proponent of sound financial-management strategies when he put into place the systems he and his team badly needed in order to safeguard and grow his portfolio.

For investors like Dan, where there's a will, there's a way. As Dan progressed as an investor, he made mistakes and hit roadblocks, some of which held potentially devastating consequences. Each time he met one of these problems, Dan turned it into an opportunity to provide a solution to strengthen his business. So read, learn and remember: success is a process.

* * *

When Dan Heon's accountant told him he planned to retire, Dan set about hiring a new one so he could transition from one to the other. He talked to other real estate investors, and then gave the accountants he'd been referred to a call. As a mortgage broker and real estate investor who values customer service, Dan saw that first phone contact as a kind of test. If an accountant didn't return his call within a week, Dan took him or her off his list, figuring they were too busy or didn't want his business. With those who did call back, he chatted for five to ten minutes and set up face-to-face meetings with the professionals whose answers he liked the most. Those meetings lasted about 30 minutes, focused on business generalities and allowed Dan and the accountant interview each other. It was a thorough process, and it accomplished Dan's primary goal — to find the right accountant who had experience in investment real estate.

That kind of attention to detail wasn't there when Dan started investing about 15 years ago. A diesel mechanic with a well-paying union job, Dan got into investing because he was frustrated by the dollars and no-sense reality of his job situation. He'd worked hard to get a full-time position on the same shop floor where he'd completed his apprenticeship, only to find himself surrounded and astounded by what he now calls a "union mentality." With pay based on seniority versus merit, Dan was stuck making the same money as the guy across the work bench. Only the other guy had been there 20 years. No wonder he thought night shifts included a little nap time on the company payroll!

Determined to take control of a better future for himself, Dan started investing in real estate. He arranged his work life so he could focus on his financial future and his investment real estate at the same time. That was a smart move, since banks are amenable to an investor who has a full-time job, as that provides some welcome security for loans.

Using seller financing, whereby the seller of a property provides the loan, he bought his first few houses with his sights trained on growing his portfolio to create short-term cash flow and long-term wealth. He bought more property as soon as he had money in the bank. In hindsight, his predilection for growth wasn't so smart. Dan's portfolio was growing, but he wasn't keeping track of how much money he owed and how soon loans had to be paid back. Working without a real business plan or a tax strategy, he eventually faced a dire truth: he had six months to repay $200,000 to private lenders. Dan weighed his options. He could sell everything, pay back his lenders and pay taxes on the capital gains to the government, then start over. Or, he could find a way to raise the cash he owed his creditors.

Option two was complicated, but since he wasn't keen on starting over or on paying tax and keeping nothing for himself, Dan became a mortgage broker, specializing in mortgages for people who wanted to buy real estate for their own investment portfolios. He also started to attract a considerable amount of RRSP money to real estate investments. "The whole plan came from knowing that investors like me needed more creative ways to finance their real estate purchases," recalls Dan. With his creditors paid, Dan then took an honest look at his time on the brink of economic disaster — and vowed never to let himself get into that situation again.

By late 2009, Dan's own real estate company had purchased more than 75 properties. More impressive than the steady growth of a sustainable investment portfolio is Dan's willingness to mentor novice investors through some of the same management and organizational issues he encountered in his early investment days. He's also willing to share his experience with more complicated real estate development deals and regardless of whether he's talking about hiring an accountant or putting together a multi-million dollar deal, Dan's biggest message targets the need to build a team:

Sophisticated investors take responsibility for the fact that they need other people to help them do the things they want to do.

Without that expertise, novice investors waste valuable time reinventing wheels which are likely to fall off over time, says Dan.

Behind the Team

On the financial management and tax strategy front, Dan backs up his focus on team by reminding investors that success is in the following details:

1. **Seek peer support so you can learn from the success of others.**

A proponent of what he calls "the power of the group," Dan also encourages newbies to join a local chapter of REIN. His own experience with doing this helped him learn the proven systems sophisticated investors had already adopted. Being surrounded by people in the know, continues to help him navigate the many variables associated with changing markets. A few years ago, Dan still self-managed a few properties close to home. When the market changed dramatically in 2008, he hired professionals. "In a good market, you have ten people beating down your door to rent a property and you pick the best one. In a tougher market, you have to do more creative ads and keep on top of what people are looking for in a rental property and where they want to live. I really don't have time to do that, so I'll let a professional help me weather this period," notes Dan.

2. **Adopt a good bookkeeping system.**

You should have a bookkeeping system in place before, or be developing it concurrently with, the purchase of your first property. This is the best way to keep track of what you own and what you owe. "If you don't know where your business is at financially, you're running blind," says Dan. "Having the right accountant and the right bookkeeper in place was like installing a navigator or GPS for my business." If you don't get the information you need from your bookkeeping and accounting systems, look for ways to change them.

3. Be diligent and don't let things fall through the cracks.

Everyone makes mistakes, says Dan. "I was so disorganized and the problems I faced with creditors literally forced me to become a broker and take my business in another direction. If you don't want to do that, don't let yourself get into that kind of situation." Never guess at your financial situation. It is better to know and make decisions based on reality.

4. Remember that you get what you pay for.

You can't act on what you don't know and when it comes to tax strategies, Dan admits there's an awful lot he doesn't know, and neither does he have the time to learn it. He's listened to a lot of novice investors say they can't afford quality legal or accounting services. Dan tells them they're dead wrong. And the proof is in the rebate cheque: Dan recently got a $16,000 rebate he didn't expect and he credits that cash directly to his accountant's expertise.

"I know it's tough to look at what's coming in and out of your business and still say 'this service is worth it.' But unless you really know how to write and follow a business plan and develop long-term tax strategies, you're going to need good advice on an ongoing basis. Without it, your business can't grow."

* * *

ACTION STEPS

✓ What two components of your real estate business are the largest users of your time, or give you the most frustration? Who do you know who could help you do a better job of running your investment business? When will you contact that person?

✓ Once you know what you need to do, don't skip steps, even in a booming market.

✓ Review your system from top to bottom at least once a year. This is like an athletic training camp. Review and practice the basics so the steps become automatic. This minimizes mistakes.

✓ Forget about knowing it all. You will never know it all and you don't need to. That is your professional's job.

✓ Don't worry about making mistakes. No matter how good you are, you will make some errors. Focus on continuous improvement.

✓ Remember that "systems" do not need to be computer-based or formal. They do need to increase efficiency and be effective. Just make sure they are proven and help you achieve what you are trying to create.

ⓘ INVESTOR-IN-ACTION: NAVAZ MURJI

Add knowledge and experience to your bench.

Navaz Murji's experience as a real estate investor really offers two key lessons. They are: 1) if you want to be an investor, you need to take action; and 2) if you lack knowledge and expertise, get it from someone else who knows. Today, these lessons are the crux of Navaz's investment business and accounting practice.

As a professionally trained accountant who wanted to transfer his financial expertise to the real estate investment business, Navaz had to learn how to get out of his own way! This is not an unusual situation to find yourself in when you come to real estate investing from a professional background (such as accountants and engineers). In professions like these, risk-management decisions are often based solely on an assessment of your own skills. (Can this be done? Do I know how to do it?)

Real estate investment demands that you climb out of that box and deliberately seek input from people whose knowledge and experience are significantly different from your own. Before he got into investing, for example, Navaz already knew how to read and assess documents like balance sheets, cash flow statements and statements of shareholders' equity (see Tip #6). He could also walk clients from his accounting practice through the tax implications of decisions like how they document receipts, pay employees (including family members), claim property repairs and maintenance costs, or claim vehicle expenses and purchases, all of which are detailed in Part 3 of this book.

Where Navaz's expertise held him back was his inability to think outside the box in the context of risk. For Navaz to become a successful real estate investor, he needed to learn how to manage risk in a different way. The Property Goldmine Score Card and REIN Property Analyzer Form (see Appendices) helped him find the right properties to buy. A commitment to "doing the extra 10% that others won't" helped him fine-tune investment and management strategies. No longer tentative and held back by what some call "analysis paralysis," Navaz got serious about investing — and serious about always being on the lookout for ways to improve and grow his investment business.

Want a closer look at an investor-in-action? Here's his story.

* * *

Navaz Murji thought his advice was helpful when he urged his parents to buy a home in Edmonton soon after the family emigrated from the East African country of Tanzania in 1979. A couple of years later, Navaz, the fifth of six children, found himself helping his dad make payments as interest rates skyrocketed. "I was on the hook. I'd talked him into it and my dad was working minimum-wage jobs," recalls Navaz, who was in his early twenties at the time. Worrisome as the situation was, he also watched his father pay off that property by the early 1990s and move into his retirement years with relative ease. "There was a time in my life when I said I'd never buy residential property again. But then I saw what it helped my parents do and I knew real estate investment was important to long-term wealth."

That lesson was driven home by the people Navaz was meeting through his work as a certified general accountant. "My dad always told me to go to school, work hard and you'll do well. I did that, but I was meeting clients who didn't have much in terms of formal education, but had a ton of money through real estate."

If that was Lesson One, then Lesson Two was learning the difference between knowing what you want to do and doing it well. "I bought my first real estate investment property in 1997," says Navaz. Now a certified general accountant living in Burnaby, B.C., he bought a single-family dwelling in nearby Surrey. "I didn't have a plan. I didn't understand the market and I sure didn't understand how the type of property affected cash flow."

Still possessing a vision of successful real estate investment, Navaz started reading more about the business and took his first formal real estate course. Looking back, Navaz knows he was on the right track, even though those early attempts to get smarter weren't paying off. He now recognizes there is no point spending money on courses based on U.S. information. (His own accounting background made that very clear. "I knew you could not do the things they were telling Canadian investors to do," recalls Navaz.) He was also frustrated by the way some programs claimed to include "investment coaching" when all he got was a regular phone call from a "secretary who wanted to see if I'd done anything that week." Worse, the courses always seemed to promise success — as long as you kept buying more programs.

Still, Navaz was taking action. By early 2000, he owned a 25-unit multi-family building and started buying properties in Prince George,

Vancouver and Kamloops, eventually building a portfolio of single-family properties.

Through all of the acquisitions, however, it didn't seem like the vision of success was any closer, says Navaz. When he and his wife Rozmin sold their own home to buy a multi-family property, their three children were still living at home. In addition to the hassles of finding themselves back in the rental housing market, property management issues on the single-family front cost him hours in travel time as the property was located in another province. Through all of this, he also had to balance the demands of a busy accounting practice.

Seeking a new direction, a better plan and an unbiased view of the real estate market, Navaz joined REIN in late 2005. By then, he'd sold the multi-family building so he and Rozmin could buy another primary residence. Now focused on consolidating his workload and creating more free time, he divested most of the properties in Vancouver, Kamloops and Prince George and set a fresh course, this time, with REIN as his rudder.

"The information I was getting from REIN was very black-and-white. This is how you do your due diligence on a property. This is how you identify quality tenants. REIN helped me make decisions better and faster. I was able to take action with confidence."

By February 2006, he'd bought his first multi-family building in Edmonton and he added three more properties over four months. When his father took ill that same year, Navaz backed off the acquisitions to spend more time with his family. By 2008, he'd bought a few more single-family homes, all with positive cash flow. "It's at the point where I don't need more. But if a decent deal comes through, I'll be looking."

Now able to travel for several weeks a year, he's also investigating quality franchise businesses for his three adult children to buy and he's quick to credit real estate investment for giving him the financial means to spend more time enjoying life and still help his children.

Successful but Still Learning
A changing real estate market also has him thinking about starting a public company to invest in real estate. This time, he'll launch that journey with a team of people (like securities lawyers and accountants) who understand

the legal side of that enterprise. "I will bring in people who know how to do this. I need new people on the team."

Backed by experience, his advice to those thinking about real estate investment comes quick and blunt:

1. Educate yourself.
2. Let income drive your investment decisions (not income tax avoidance!).
3. Don't get caught by analysis paralysis.
4. Find people who can help you do what you want to do. Build a team.

"The biggest stumbling block for me was my own mindset. At first, I spent too much time thinking about what could go wrong. And then when I did take action, I complicated things with some kind of bad choices."

On the upside, "I didn't quit. I found ways to stay the course. And boy, am I ever glad now."

* * *

ACTION STEPS

✓ Think about what holds you back from making decisions and rate the following (1 being most important and 5 of minor importance).
  – Level of risk
  – Fear of making a mistake
  – Having enough information
  – Having done it before
  – Not knowing or having confidence in what you're doing
  – Afraid of looking bad in front of others
  – Fear of losing money
✓ Think about what analysis paralysis costs you. Be honest. Analysis paralysis can keep us from taking advantage of good deals. It can also keep us mired in problems we should be solving (by improving properties, focusing only on quality tenants, hiring a bookkeeper, etc.).

Remember: Fear is essential to survival. But risk can be managed. Talk to professionals and surround yourself with like-minded thinkers whose own success has meant overcoming fear and self-doubt.

✓ Stop making excuses. When faced with a "reason" to not take action, write it down. Is it an excuse based on fear? Physically cross it out with your pen. Now turn the excuse into a positive action message. Here's how to use that approach with fears about bookkeeping and taxes.

Fear: I don't know anyone who would be able to put my books in order.

Positive Message: I know other real estate investors. I can talk to them about how they found their bookkeepers and how they put their books in order.

Fear: I don't what receipts to keep and what to throw out.

Positive Message: I'm not the first real estate investor! Who can help me fine-tune my record-keeping system?

APPENDICES

- PROPERTY GOLDMINE SCORE CARD
- REIN PROPERTY ANALYZER FORM
- CANADIAN REAL ESTATE GLOSSARY

PROPERTY GOLDMINE SCORE CARD

Property Address: _____

Town: _____ Prov: _____

Source: _____ Tel:_____

Property-Specific Questions

❑ Can you change the use of the property?
❑ Can you buy it substantially below retail market value?
❑ Can you substantially increase the current rents?
❑ Can you do small renovations to substantially increase the value?

Area's Economic Influences

❑ Is there an <u>overall increase in demand</u> in the area?
❑ Are there currently <u>sales over list price</u> in the area?
❑ Is there a noted <u>increase in labour and materials cost</u> in the area?
❑ Is there a lot of <u>speculative investment</u> in the area?
❑ Is it <u>an area in transition</u> — moving upwards in quality?
❑ Is there a major <u>transportation improvement</u> occurring nearby?
❑ Is it in an area that is going to benefit from the ripple effect?
❑ Has the <u>political leadership</u> created a growth atmosphere?
❑ Is the area's <u>average income</u> increasing faster than the provincial average?
❑ Is it an area that is attractive to the baby boomers?
❑ Is the area <u>growing faster</u> than the provincial average?
❑ Are <u>interest rates</u> at historic lows and/or moving downwards?

_____ = Total ✓ s

Does This Property Fit Your System?   ❑ yes ❑ no
Does It Take You Closer To Your Goal?   ❑ yes ❑ no

REIN PROPERTY ANALYZER FORM

Property Data:

Address: _____ City/Area: _____ Date Viewed: _____

Asking Price $ _____ Size (sq ft): _____ Age: _____

Major Repairs: _____ Est Repair Cost $ _____

Owner: _____ Tel: _____ Fax: _____

Source: _____ Tel: _____ Fax: _____

Overall Condition: 1 2 3 4 5

Income & Inspection:

Suite # or Desc	# of Bedrooms	Current Rent	Projected Rent	Increase Date	Inspection Comments

Total Monthly Rent $_____ $_____

Total Annual Rent $_____ $_____

Expenses:

	Current Annual	Current Monthly	Projected Monthly	Comments
Heat (gas, oil, elect, hot water, other _____)				Paid by Tenant / Landlord
Electricity				Paid by Tenant / Landlord
Water/Sewer				Paid by Tenant / Landlord / Condo
Taxes				Included in Mortgage Payment?
Condo Fee				Last Increase date:
Insurance				
Property Management	%			Current Management Rating 1 2 3 4 5
Vacancy Allowance	%			Current Vacancy _____%
Rental Pool Mgmt	%			
Repairs & Maintenance	%			Overall Condition 1 2 3 4 5
Resident Manager				Current On-site Impression 1 2 3 4 5
Other:				

TOTAL MONTHLY $_____ $_____

TOTAL MONTHLY INCOME less TOTAL MONTHLY EXPENSES (Before Debt Service)=

Current: $ _____   Projected: $ _____

TOTAL PROJECTED INCOME $_____

Mortgaging/Debt Service:

	Balance	Interest Rate	Expiry Date	Monthly Payment
1st Mortgage		%		P I T
2nd Mortgage		%		P I T
Vendor Take Back		%		P I T
Other		%		P I T

TOTAL DEBT SERVICE $_____

NET CASH FLOW $_____

Purchase Details:

PROJECTED PURCHASE PRICE $_____

     1st Mortgage Funding   ($_____)
     2nd Mortgage Funding   ($_____)
     Vendor Take Back   ($_____)
     Other Funding   ($_____)

TOTAL DEBT FUNDING   ($_____)
DOWN PAYMENT REQUIRED $_____

Purchase Costs:

     Professional Inspection $_____
     Value Appraisal $_____
     Real Property Report (Survey) $_____
     Mortgage Set-Up Costs $_____
     Mortgage Broker Fees $_____
     Legal Costs (incl disbursements) $_____
     Staying Power Fund $_____
     Immediate Repairs $_____
     Immediate Renovations $_____
     Other _____ $_____
     Other _____ $_____

TOTAL PURCHASE COSTS $_____

TOTAL CASH REQUIRED TO CLOSE (Down payment + Purchase costs) $_____

1. Does this property take me closer to my goal or farther away?   ❏ Closer   ❏ Farther
2. Does this property fit my system?   ❏ Yes   ❏ No
3. Will this property be impeccably property managed?   ❏ Yes   ❏ No
4. Who will manage the property?   _____

CANADIAN REAL ESTATE GLOSSARY

A

ABSTRACT OF TITLE
A written history of the title to a parcel of real estate as recorded in a Land Registry Office.

ACCELERATION CLAUSE
A clause in the mortgage document that accelerates the maturity date and states that upon default, the principal sum of the mortgage and accrued interest falls due.

ACCRUED INTEREST
Interest that has accumulated unpaid since the last payment date.

ADD-ON INTEREST
An interest amount added to the principal of a debt and made payable as part of the debt, usually in equal periodic installments (also called pre-calculated interest).

ADJUSTABLE RATE MORTGAGE (ARM)
A mortgage for which the interest rate is adjusted periodically according to movements in a pre-selected index.

ADJUSTMENT DATE
The date regarded as the official beginning of a mortgage.

AFFIDAVIT
A statement of declaration in writing and sworn or affirmed before an authorized individual, such as a notary public.

AGENCY
A relationship that arises out of a contract, where an agent is authorized by a principal to engage in certain acts, usually in dealing with one or more third parties.

AGREEMENT OF PURCHASE AND SALE
A written contract to buy property in which the purchaser and vendor agree to sell upon terms and conditions as set forth in the agreement.

ALIENATION CLAUSE
This is a clause that enables the mortgagee to demand payment of the outstanding balance including interest upon sale or transfer of title (also known as a "due-on-sale" clause).

AMORTIZATION
The gradual retirement of a debt by means of partial payments of the principal at regular intervals.

AMORTIZATION OF A MORTGAGE
The arrangement for paying off a mortgage by installments over a period of time.

AMORTIZATION PERIOD
The time period required to completely retire a debt through scheduled payments of principal.

ANNIVERSARY DATE
The occasion of one year from an event pertaining to a mortgage, e.g., the registration date.

ANNUAL BUDGET
Now required by the *Condominium Property Act*, this budget is the basis upon which contributions are levied and funds collected.

ANNUAL GENERAL MEETING (AGM)
Once per year, within 15 months of the last one, a condominium board is required to convene an Annual General Meeting of unit owners.

ANNUAL PERCENTAGE RATE (APR)
The yearly interest percentage of a mortgage as expressed by the actual rate of interest paid, given the term, rate, amount and cost of arrangement.

APPRAISED VALUE
An estimate of property value written by a qualified individual (AACI). Appraisals performed for mortgage lending purposes may not reflect the market value of the property, or the purchase price.

APPROVED LENDER
Lending institution authorized by the government of Canada through Canada Mortgage and

Housing Corporation (CMHC) to make loans under the terms of the *National Housing Act*; only approved lenders can negotiate mortgages that require mortgage loan insurance.

APPURTENANCE
Something that is outside the property itself, but belongs to the land and is joined thereto; e.g., a road over another's land providing an access (right-of-way) is an appurtenance.

ARREARS
To be "in arrears" is to be behind in the payments called for under a mortgage agreement.

ASSESSED VALUE
An amount assigned to a taxable property for the purpose of equalizing the burden of taxation.

ASSIGNEE
One who takes the rights or title of another by assignment.

ASSIGNMENT
The method by which a purchase and sale contract is transferred between two parties (for a consideration or fee).

ASSIGNMENT OF MORTGAGE
The assigning of a mortgagee's interest in the mortgage to a new mortgagee. The legal sale of the mortgage with or without an agreement to repurchase.

ASSIGNMENT OF RENTALS
The enforceable diversion of income from a mortgaged property to the mortgagee.

ASSIGNOR
One who transfers or assigns the rights or title to another.

ASSUMABILITY
A feature of a mortgage that allows the buyer to take over the seller's mortgage on the property.

ASSUMPTION AGREEMENT
A document that binds someone other than the mortgagor to perform mortgage obligations.

ASSUMPTION OF MORTGAGE
The action of a purchaser taking responsibility for a mortgage debt by way of a legal agreement. The original covenanter(s)' responsibility pursuant to the mortgage obligation remains intact

in such arrangement, so long as the existing documentation remains registered.

ATTORNMENT OF RENT
The redirection of rental income to a mortgagee, usually in the event of default.

AUTHORITY
The legal right given by a principal to an agent to act on the principal's behalf in performing specific acts or negotiations.

AVERAGING
Sometimes called "levelling." This is the calculation made to determine the interest when a second mortgage is taken out; averaging determines the average interest rate of the two mortgages.

B

BALANCE DUE ON COMPLETION
The amount of money a purchaser will be required to pay to the vendor to complete the purchase after all adjustments have been made.

BALLOON PAYMENT
This is a final mortgage payment at the end of the term that pays off the outstanding loan in full. The amount of money (principal) required to discharge a mortgage at maturity.

BARELAND CONDOMINIUM
In traditional condominiums, both the master lot and the walls and roofs of the buildings are common property. In bareland condominiums, only the land is condominiumized, and the structures are the responsibility of the owners.

BIRD DOG
A person who looks for properties that fit your guidelines and brings them to you for a fee.

BLANKET MORTGAGE
A single registered document that encumbers more than one property.

BLENDED PAYMENT
Equal payments consisting of both principal and interest, paid regularly during the term of the mortgage.

BOARD OF DIRECTORS
Every Condominium Corporation must have a board of directors, which is responsible for

the proper administration of the condominium and the bylaws.

BREACH OF CONTRACT
Failure to fulfill an obligation under a contract. Breach confers a right of action on the offended party.

BRIDGE OR INTERIM LOANS (MORTGAGES)
Interim loans are used to bridge the gap between the initial construction and the first advances available under the terms of the construction mortgage. Interim loans can also be used for financing between phases of construction, until the construction is completed to a stage whereby the mortgagee lender will advance funds to pay for the phase of the construction. Usually, when the mortgage is advanced, the proceeds of the mortgage are used to return the bridge or interim financing. Bridge financing is also used when a sale closes after a purchaser takes possession on a purchase.

BROKER
A person licensed by the provincial or territorial government to trade in real estate. Brokers may form companies of offices that appoint sales representatives to provide services to the seller or buyer, or they may provide the same services themselves; also referred to as agents.

BUILDING CODES
Regulations established by government providing for structural requirements.

BUILDING PERMIT
Certificate that must be obtained from the municipality by the property owner or contractor before a building can be erected or repaired; it must be posted in a conspicuous place until the job is completed and passed as satisfactory by a municipal building inspector.

BUYDOWN
A payment to the lender from the seller, buyer or third party causing the lender to reduce the interest rate during the term of the mortgage.

BUYER BROKERAGE AGREEMENT
Written agreement between the buyer and the buyer's agent, outlining the agency relationship between the two parties, and the manner in which the buyer's agent will be compensated.

BUYER'S AGENT
Person or firm representing the buyer; primary allegiance is to the buyer.

BY-LAWS
A set of rules and procedures adopted by a special resolution of unit-owners for the administration of the condominium corporation. Each condominium corporation has its own special by-laws.

C

CANADA MORTGAGE AND HOUSING CORPORATION (CMHC)
A Canadian Crown Corporation that administers the *National Housing Act*. CMHC services include the insuring of high-ratio mortgage loans for lenders.

CAP
Refers to a maximum interest rate increase for a mortgage.

CAPITAL GAIN OR LOSS
The difference between the base price (cost plus purchase expenses) and the sale price of a capital asset.

CAPITALIZATION RATE
The rate of return anticipated by an investor in a property.

CAPITALIZED VALUE
The value of a property based on the net income.

CAVEAT EMPTOR
"Let the buyer beware." A buyer must fully examine the product or service he or she is buying before making the purchase.

CERTIFICATE OF CHARGE
A mortgage document in the Land Titles System.

CESSATION OF CHARGE
A discharge of a mortgage in the Land Titles System.

CHAIN OF TITLE
The sequence of conveyances and encumbrances affecting a title to land from the time that the original patent was granted or as far back as records are available.

CHARGE
The name given to a mortgage document when title is registered under the *Land Titles Act*.

CHATTEL MORTGAGE
An encumbrance against moveable possessions or personal property that may be removed without damage to the property, e.g., appliances.

CHATTELS
Moveable possessions and personal property that may be removed without damage to the property, e.g., appliances.

CLOSED MORTGAGE
A reference to the absence of the privilege to accelerate repayment during the term of a mortgage either by bulk payment(s) or increase to scheduled remittances. A penalty applies if you repay the loan in full before the end of a closed term.

CLOSING
See "Date of Completion"; the day the legal title to the property changes hands.

CLOSING COSTS
Costs in addition to the purchase price of the home, such as legal fees, transfer fees and disbursements, that are payable on the closing date; they typically range from 1.5–4 percent of a home's selling price.

CLOSING DATE
The date on which the buyer takes over the property.

CLOUD ON TITLE
Any encumbrance or claim that affects title to property.

COLLATERAL MORTGAGE
A mortgage that secures a loan given by way of a promissory note; the money that is borrowed can be used to buy a property or for another purpose such as home renovation or a vacation.

COLLATERAL SECURITY
An additional form of security, pledged to reduce the risk of a mortgagee.

COMMISSION
Amount agreed to by the seller and the real estate broker/agent and stated in the listing agreement and payable to the broker/agent on closing.

COMMITMENT
A written notice from a lender who advises of approval to advance a specified amount of funds under certain conditions.

COMMON LAW
That part of the law formulated, developed and administered by the old common law courts, based originally on unwritten common customs.

COMMON PROPERTY
Every part of the condominium plan that is not a unit is common property. The condominium corporation is responsible for the maintenance and service of the common property.

COMPLETION LOAN
A mortgage loan disbursed following the satisfactory completion of construction.

COMPOUND INTEREST
Interest on both the principal and on interest that has accrued.

COMPONENT FINANCING
A device by which lending is split into separate parts and treated individually.

COMPS (Comparables)
A listing of comparable properties used to value a similar property. Often used in appraisals.

CONDITION PRECEDENT
An event or action necessary before an agreement becomes binding.

CONDITION SUBSEQUENT
A condition referring to a future event upon the happening of which the contract becomes no longer binding on the parties.

CONDITIONAL OFFER
Offer to purchase that is subject to specified conditions; usually a stipulated time limit within which the specified conditions must be met.

CONDOMINIUM
The ownership of a separate amount of space in a multiple dwelling or other multiple-ownership

of common elements used jointly with other owners.

CONDOMINIUM FEE
A monthly common payment among owners that is allocated to pay expenses.

CONSIDERATION
Something of value given to make a promise of repayment enforceable.

CONSTANT ANNUAL PERCENT
The percentage required to pay the principal and interest to amortize a loan.

CONSTANT PAYMENT MORTGAGE
A mortgage that is paid by equal periodic amounts consisting of principal and interest payments. It may be self-liquidating, which means the mortgage is entirely paid off at maturity (fully amortized), or partially amortized, at the end of which there remains a principal balance due at maturity (also known as balloon mortgage).

CONSTRUCTION ADVANCE
Moneys advanced to the borrower under a construction loan.

CONSTRUCTION LIEN
A claim against property pursuant to labour, services or materials supplied.

CONSTRUCTION LOAN
A short-term loan made to a builder for construction of buildings, usually to be paid out by another mortgage upon final completion. Also, a description used in reference to a mortgage that is advanced in pre-determined stages, according to the amount of work completed.

CONSTRUCTION LOAN AGREEMENT
An agreement between a lender and a builder setting out terms of an agreement — loan amount, rate, method of drawing funds and conditions for advancing.

CONTRACT
An agreement between two or more parties given receipt of lawful consideration to do or refrain from doing some act.

CONVENTIONAL MORTGAGE
A mortgage loan that does not exceed 75 percent of the lending value of the property. Mortgages that exceed this limit must be insured by CMHC (or similar insurance provider).

CONVEYANCE
The transfer of property ownership. Also, the written instrument whereby such transfer is effected. Conveyance includes a mortgage, charge and lease, etc.

CO-OPERATIVE
The ownership of a separate amount of space in a multiple dwelling or multiple-occupancy building with proportioned tenancy in common ownership of common elements. It's used jointly with other owners; however, the owner does not have clear title to a specific unit but becomes a shareholder of the corporation, which owns all of the property and occupies by way of a tenancy agreement subject to shareholder agreement administered by an elected board of directors.

COVENANT
An agreement contained in an instrument creating an obligation. It may be positive, stipulating the performance of some act. It may be negative or restrictive, forbidding the commission of some act. A clause in a legal document which, in the case of a mortgage, gives the parties to the mortgage a right or an obligation; for example, a covenant can impose the obligation on a borrower to make mortgage payments in certain amounts on certain dates; a mortgage document consists of covenants agreed to by the borrower and the lender.

CROSS-COLLATERALIZATION
A reference to security involving various liens held in support of one or more advances made by a lender to a borrower.

D

DAMAGES
Compensation or indemnity for loss owing to breach of contract.

DATE OF COMPLETION
The date specified by an agreement of purchase and sale, when the purchaser is to deliver the balance of money due and the vendor to deliver a duly executed deed.

DEBT SERVICE
The amount of principal and interest payments made under a mortgage.

DEBT-SERVICE RATIO
Measurement of debt payments to gross household income.

DEFAULT
Failure to abide by the terms of a mortgage loan agreement. Failure to make mortgage payments (defaulting) may give cause to the mortgagor to take legal action to possess (foreclose on) the mortgaged property.

DEFERRED INCOME
An accounting method of dealing with income that is received but not included in a statement of earnings as normal earnings.

DEFICIENCY
An insufficient payment, often relating to an amount recovered under a power of sale or foreclosure action.

DEFLATION
A decline in the general level of prices; or an increase in the value of money; or an increase in the amount of money in circulation.

DELAYED PARTICIPATION LOAN
Where a lender disposes of a loan to several other participants putting up their respective shares later.

DEMAND NOTE
Payment is made on demand, usually within a few days' notice to the borrower.

DEPOSIT
Payment of money or other valuable consideration as a pledge for fulfillment of contract. Money placed in trust by the purchaser when an offer to purchase is made; the sum is held by the real estate representative or lawyer until the sale is closed, then paid to the vendor.

DEPRECIATED REPRODUCTION COST
Appraisal method by which the cost of replacing a structure, minus depreciation, gives the depreciation reproduction cost.

DEPRECIATION
A loss in value due to any cause.

DISCHARGE OF MORTGAGE
A document executed by the mortgagee, and given to the mortgagor when a mortgage loan has been repaid in full before, at or after the maturity date.

DISCLOSURE STATEMENT
A statement contained in a consumer credit transaction in order to disclose complete credit terms and interest rates.

DISCOUNT
Reduction in product price or cost of a service. A discount is the difference between the nominal face value of a loan and the actual cash received by the borrower, because interest is paid at the beginning of a loan based on the sum to be repaid at maturity.

DISCOUNTED CASH-FLOW ANALYSIS
This is a method of analysis that calculates the true value of an investment in terms of the present value, i.e., what the investment is worth now, although it is spread over a number of years. To compensate for future earnings a discount factor is added in so that a real comparison can be made between an investment with quick return and one that is placed over a number of years.

DISCOUNTED LOAN
The face value of the loan minus the interest or discount charged by the lender is the amount actually advanced to a borrower.

DOMINANT TENEMENT
The estate that derives benefit from an easement over a subservient estate, as in a right-of-way.

DOWER INTEREST
A wife's interest in the lands of her husband accruing to her by virtue of the marriage.

DOWN PAYMENT
The portion of the house price the buyer must pay up front from personal resources before securing a mortgage; it usually ranges from 5 to 25% of the purchase price.

DOWNSIDE LEVERAGE
Occurs where the debt service on a mortgage exceeds the yield on an investor's property, thereby reducing cash flow.

DRAWEE
The person, bank or corporation from whom a bill, note or cheque is drawn and from whom payment is expected by the payee or his assignee.

DRAWER
The person or corporation who writes a cheque or note for payment to a third party. In the case of a bill of exchange, the drawer is the creditor and is usually the payee.

DUAL AGENT
A real estate broker/agent who acts as agent for both buyer and seller in the same transaction.

DUE ON SALE CLAUSE
A mortgage clause that states that if the property is sold, the mortgage cannot be assumed by the new purchaser without qualification. The mortgage becomes immediately due and payable upon the sale of the property.

E

EASEMENT
The right acquired for access over another person's land for a specific purpose, such as for a driveway or public utilities.

ECONOMIC DEPRECIATION
Loss in value of property due to external influences related to the property, i.e., not controlled by the owner.

EFFECTIVE GROSS INCOME
The estimated gross income less allowances for vacancies and rent losses.

EFFECTIVE INTEREST RATE
The actual interest rate on investment where a debt or loan was bought at a discount or at a premium.

ENCROACHMENT
A fixture, such as a wall or fence, which illegally intrudes into or invades on public or private property, thus diminishing the size and value of the invaded property.

ENCUMBRANCE
Outstanding claim or lien recorded against a property, e.g., a mortgage, or any legal right to the use of the property by another person who is not the owner.

END LOAN
The mortgage loan to the final customer, such as a purchaser of a condominium unit.

EQUITABLE MORTGAGE
The transfer of equity in property as security for a debt. Any mortgage registered after the first mortgage.

EQUITY
The value of real estate over and above the mortgage(s) against it.

EQUITY OF REDEMPTION
The right of the mortgagor to reclaim clear title to the real property upon full repayment of the debt.

ESCROW ACCOUNT (American term)
An account held by an agent on behalf of his principal for the payment of money due to a third party on the event of specified incidents, e.g., a vendor's solicitor will hold funds on his behalf until title deeds to a property have been delivered and the property has been registered and the keys delivered to the purchaser; or an account maintained by a mortgagee for the payment of property taxes or life insurance premiums.

ESTATE
The degree, quantity, nature and extent of interest that a person has in real property.

ESTOPPEL CERTIFICATE (Renter confirmation)
A written statement or certificate that states certain facts upon which the receiver of the statement or a third party may rely, e.g., a lender's estoppel statement as to a purchaser or property. The lender cannot later deny the truth of these statements because a third party has relied and acted upon them.

EXACT DAY INTEREST
Interest calculated on the basis of 365 days per year or 366 days in a leap year.

EXCULPATORY CLAUSE
A clause that excuses one party from personal liability in the event of a default.

EXPROPRIATION
The act of forcefully taking private property for public use.

EXTENSION AGREEMENT
The lengthening of a term on a contract to extend the maturity date; or to permit more time

for the performance of an obligation or condition; or the extension of the coverage of a lien to include more property.

F

FEASIBILITY ANALYSIS
An analysis to determine the feasibility of a project. Details of construction costs, projected income from the project plus location and economic factors affecting the project will be required. Similar to a feasibility study by a developer conducted to decide whether to proceed with plans and required by the lender to decide whether to provide funds.

FEE SIMPLE
The highest estate or absolute right in real property. In common law, the most common way real estate is owned. The most complete ownership interest one can have in real property.

FINAL ORDER OF CLOSURE
Judgment taken against a mortgagor, extinguishing the equity of redemption.

FINANCING STATEMENT
A statement filed by a creditor in a public records office identifying the parties, giving their addresses and describing the collateral.

FIRST MORTGAGE
The mortgage agreement that has first claim on the property in the event of default.

FIRST MORTGAGE BOND
Bonds issued by a corporation secured upon the property and earnings of the issuing corporation.

FIXED-RATE MORTGAGE
This is the usual form of mortgage, where the interest rate remains the same during the entire life of the term.

FIXTURES
Permanent improvements to property that may not be removed at the expiration of the term of lease or tenure.

FLAT PAYMENT
An all-inclusive monthly payment that is calculated to include principal, interest and taxes. Under this system there is no specific breakdown as to the amounts of the principal, interest and taxes.

FLOATING RATE OF INTEREST
Rate of interest that fluctuates according to prime lending rates, e.g., 2 percent above prime rate is usually chargeable on short-term loans such as construction loans.

FLOOR TO CEILING LOAN
A permanent loan or advance made in two stages, (a) on completion of construction according to agreed-upon terms and conditions, and (b) the balance advanced upon occupancy or upon cash-flow requirements.

FORECLOSURE
Remedial court action taken by a mortgagee when default occurs on a mortgage, to cause forfeiture of the equity of redemption of the mortgagor.

FORWARD COMMITMENT
Lender's commitment to make or assume a future loan.

FREEHOLD
The ownership of a tract of land on which the building(s) are located. The oldest and most common type of ownership of real estate.

FULLY AMORTIZED LOAN
A mortgage loan wherein the stipulated payments repay the loan in full by its maturity date.

FURTHER CHARGE
A second or subsequent loan of money to a mortgagor by a mortgagee, either on the same or on an additional security.

G

G/E CAPITAL
The General Electric Capital Corporation insures high-ratio mortgages for lenders.

GALE DATES
The dates on which interest is charged or compounded on the mortgage loan.

GAP FINANCING
A loan required by a builder to obtain funds during the period between a permanent take out commitment and a construction loan. The construction lender will usually require permanent mortgage commitment to the full amount of the construction loan plus a hold-back provision that

only the "floor" amount will be funded at the completion of construction.

GENERAL CREDITOR
A creditor who has no security other than the promise of the debtor.

GRADUATED AMORTIZATION MORTGAGE
A special method of repayment on a mortgage whereby repayments in the initial period are low and are gradually stepped up at a higher rate. Graduated payment mortgages were devised to enable lower income families to become home-owners.

GRANT
A technical term used in deeds of conveyance to indicate a transfer of an interest or estate in land.

GRANTEE
The party to whom an interest in real property is conveyed (the buyer).

GRANTOR
The person who conveys an interest in real estate by deed (the seller).

GROSS RENT MULTIPLIER
Method of appraising the fair market value of property by multiplying the gross rents by a factor that varies according to the type and location of the property.

GROSS DEBT SERVICE (GDS)
The percentage of gross annual income required to cover payments associated with housing. If the dwelling unit is a condo, all or a portion of common fees are included, depending on what expenses are covered.

GROSS DEBT SERVICE RATIO
Allowable ration of payments for principal, interest and taxes to gross income.

GROSS INCOME
The scheduled income from the operation of the business of management of the property, customarily stated on an annual basis.

GUARANTEED INCOME MORTGAGE
A guarantee included in a purchase money mortgage by a seller-mortgagee that there will be a minimum cash flow or net operating income

to the purchaser-mortgagee. The guarantee is limited to a short period and may be combined with a management contract whereby the seller, as manager, will operate the property.

GUARANTOR
A third party without interest in the property who agrees to assume responsibility for a debt in the event of default by the mortgagor.

H

HIGH-RATIO MORTGAGE
A mortgage loan that exceeds 80 percent of the lending value of the property and must be insured against default of payment.

HIGHEST AND BEST USE
This refers to the use of land that would most likely produce the greatest net return over a given time.

HOLDBACK
An amount of money retained by a construction lender or owner until satisfactory completion of the work performed by a contractor; a standard holdback is 10 percent of the cost of the building project.

HYPOTHECATE
To use something as security without giving up possession of it.

I

IMMEDIATE PARTICIPATION LOAN
A loan in which all of the partners contribute their share immediately.

INCOME BOND
Bonds that pay a fixed rate of interest contingent upon earnings. These bonds may originate from reorganization because of a default on mortgage bonds.

INCOME/EXPENSE RATIO
Ratio of operation expenses to gross income and expressed as a percentage (also known as operating ratio).

INCOME PROPERTY LOAN
A loan that is secured on property that already has a source of income, e.g., rents that will cover the debt service payments on the loan.

INDENTURE
A document of deed, usually in duplicate, expressing certain objects between the parties.

INFLATION
A general increase in consumer prices, most often expressed as an annual percentage rate.

INJUNCTION
A judicial process or order requiring the person to whom it is directed to do or refrain from doing a particular act.

INSTRUMENT
A form of written legal document.

INSURABLE VALUE
The term is used conventionally to designate the amount of insurance that may be carried on destructible portions of a property to indemnify the owner in the event of loss.

INTEREST ADJUSTMENT
A date from which interest on the mortgage advanced is calculated for your regular payments. This date is usually one payment period before regular mortgage payments begin, as interest payable is due from the date the mortgage is advanced.

INTEREST ESCALATION
Rate of interest on a loan is raised periodically during the term of the loan so as to encourage early repayment.

INTEREST-ONLY LOAN
Borrower pays back interest only on the loan and there is no amortization until later or until the end of the term. This may occur when a purchaser wishes to re-sell a property after a short period or if he or she wishes to build up enough income from the property before locking into a set amortization.

INTEREST RATE
The cost of a loan expressed as a percentage.

INTERIM FINANCING
Interim loans are used to bridge the gap between the construction loan and the permanent loan (hence "bridge" loans), lasting from one to three years.

INTERMEDIATE-TERM LOAN
A short-term loan from three to five years with partial or no amortization (balloon loan).

IRREVOCABLE
Incapable of being recalled or revoked; unchangeable, unalterable.

J

JOINT AND SEVERAL NOTE
Promissory note on which there are two or more promisors who are jointly and severally liable.

JOINT TENANCY
Ownership of land by two or more persons whereby, on the death of one, the survivor or survivors take the whole estate.

JUNIOR FINANCING
This is a subordinate mortgage or loan very often given by a seller of property, second in priority to an existing loan.

K

KICKER
An extra bonus or additional payment over and above the fixed interest already paid to an investor, e.g., a percentage of gross profits or cash flow.

L

LAND ACQUISITION LOAN
Loan advanced to acquire land as opposed to improving land or buildings.

LAND CONTRACT
A contract drawn between a buyer and seller for the sale of property.

LAND DEVELOPMENT LOAN
Loan advanced for the purpose of developing raw land for residential and related uses.

LAND TRANSFER TAX
A fee paid to the government for the transferring of property from seller to buyer.

LEASEHOLD
A type of interest in a property that is certain only for a specified period of time granted by contract.

LEASEHOLD APPRAISAL
A method of estimating the value of a leasehold property.

LEASEHOLD MORTGAGE
A mortgage given by a lessee on the security of the leasehold interest in the land.

LEGAL DESCRIPTION
A written description by which a property can be definitely located and which is acceptable for registration in a land registry system.

LENDING VALUE
An independent appraiser's value interpreted by the lender as to the worth of a property in the current market, given a reasonable time period to sell the property.

LESSEE
Tenant under a lease.

LESSEE'S INTEREST
The market value of a property less the value of the lessor's interest. The present worth of the annual advantage, if any, accruing to the lessee by reason of the contract rent being less than the economic rent.

LESSOR
The person who grants use of the property under lease to a tenant.

LETTER OF COMMITMENT
Letter written by the lender stating the amount of the loan, specified interest rate, term of loan and specific conditions.

LETTER OF CREDIT
Letter issued by a bank or other lending institution promising payment to a third party in accordance with the terms of the agreement. Letters of credit may be used in situations where a deposit or security is required, e.g., a builder who is about to sign a contract and has to put up security that the job will be finished, or a security deposit under a long-term lease.

LEVERAGE
Upside leverage in real estate occurs when the yield or net return on property exceeds debt service for a loan. Downside or reverse leverage occurs when the debt service is greater than the net return on investment.

LIEN
A legal claim against a property for money owed; a lien may be filed by a supplier or a subcontractor who has provided labour or materials but has not been paid; a lien must be properly filed by a claimant; it has limited life, prescribed by statute that varies from province to province; if the lien holder takes action within the prescribed time, the owner may be obliged to pay the amount claimed by the lien holder; the lien holder may force the sale of a property to pay off the debt.

LIEN HOLD BACK
A percentage of the contract price or estimated cost of work to be done, which is held back from the mortgage advance.

LINE OF CREDIT
A maximum credit limit allowed by a bank to a borrower, as long as the borrower maintains an acceptable balance on account or has a good credit rating. The terms of the credit line will vary from time to time according to the changing circumstances of the borrower or the bank.

LIS PENDENS
A legal document giving notice that an action or proceeding is pending in the courts, which affects the title to the designated property.

LIST (ASKING) PRICE
The price placed on a property for sale by the seller.

LISTING AGREEMENT
A legal agreement between the listing broker and seller, setting out the services to be rendered, describing the property for sale and stating the terms of payment; a commission is generally payable to the broker upon closing.

LOAN COVERAGE
The ratio of net operating income to debt service; in general, loan coverage of 1.3 is considered adequate for a loan-to-value ratio of 75 percent.

LOAN FEE
A charge for making a loan in addition to the interest charged to the borrower.

LOAN LOSS RESERVE
A reserve shown on a balance sheet of a real estate company as provision for any future losses in assets.

LOAN ORIGINATION
Analysis of loan applications from prospective purchasers to determine if they meet with requirements. Upon approval, the lender will issue a commitment letter.

LOAN PORTFOLIO TURNOVER
The average length of time required for the turnover of mortgage loans, i.e., until maturity.

LOAN PROCESSING
Upon application and approval of a loan, the lender has to go through a fairly standard procedure to finalize and disburse the loan, such as the setting up of files, ordering of credit reports, verification of employment and bank accounts, and so on.

LOAN-TO-VALUE RATIO
The ratio of the loan to the lending value of a property expressed as a percentage.

LOCK-IN CLAUSE
A clause that restricts prepayment of a loan during a specified period of the whole term of the mortgage. This ensures that the lender receives a stipulated return on his investment and discourages "shopping around" for another loan.

M

MARGIN OF SAFETY
A measure of the extent to which a loan is protected by property values or operating income. In the case of a mortgage, the margin of safety is the excess of equity (at fair market value) above the outstanding amount of the loan.

MARKET VALUE
The highest price estimated in terms of money that a property will bring if exposed for sale in the open market.

MARKETABLE TITLE
A title that a court of equity considers to be so free from defect that it will enforce acceptance by a purchaser.

MATURITY DATE
The last day of the term of the mortgage agreement. A mortgage loan must then be paid in full or the agreement renewed.

MECHANIC'S LIEN
A claim against the interest of the owner in a property for labour, services or materials supplied to it.

MIXED-USE DEVELOPMENT
A large-scale real estate project that is developed for a number of uses. An example of mixed-use development is a shopping centre complex.

MORATORIUM
Legislation enacted to assist debtors by postponing or suspending their contractual payments.

MORE OR LESS
Term often found in a property description intended to cover slight, unimportant or insubstantial inaccuracies to which both parties are willing to assume risk.

MORTGAGE
The legal pledge of real estate as security for a loan. Lenders consider both the property (security) and the financial worth of the borrower (covenant) in deciding on a mortgage loan.

MORTGAGE BANKER
By legislation a chartered bank authorized under the *Bank Act of Canada* to take deposits from individuals for placement in mortgages, by pooling these deposits and funding mortgages. The security for the depositor is an interest in the mortgage through the bank. A mortgage broker cannot by law pool money from individual depositors and fund mortgages, unless licensed to do so under other legislation.

MORTGAGE BOND
A bond issued by corporations and secured by a mortgage on their property.

MORTGAGE BROKER
A person who originates real estate loans and allocates mortgage funds. These funds are placed on behalf of others, through negotiation of lenders and borrowers for the best possible arrangement and satisfaction of all concerned. Licensed in Ontario by the Ministry of Financial Institutions. Could also be known as an underwriter, correspondent or investment dealer in a mortgage transaction. The mortgagor pays the broker a fee for arranging the mortgage.

MORTGAGE COMMITMENT
A formal indication by a lending institution that it will grant a mortgage loan on property, in a certain specified amount and on certain specified terms.

MORTGAGE DEBENTURE
Synonymous with mortgage bond.

MORTGAGE INSURANCE
Applies to high-ratio mortgage; the borrower arranges and pays for the insurance, which protects the lender against default if the borrower is unable to repay the mortgage.

MORTGAGE LIFE INSURANCE
Pays off the mortgage if the borrower dies.

MORTGAGE LOAN
An agreement by which a sum of money is borrowed and a promise to repay is given, wherein as a further security the borrower gives to the lender a conveyance or charge on property that he owns.

MORTGAGE NOTE
A promissory note executed in favour of the lender, giving him an encumbrance or lien on the borrower's property. A mortgagor is usually personally liable on the note.

MORTGAGE PORTFOLIO
Several mortgages held by a mortgagee, lender or broker en bloc.

MORTGAGE POSTPONEMENT
The process whereby a mortgagee may permit the borrower to renew or replace an existing mortgage that falls due prior to the maturity date of the subject mortgage.

MORTGAGEE
The lender.

MORTGAGEE IN POSSESSION
A mortgagee goes into possession by entering into actual occupation of, or by obtaining the receipt of, the rents of the mortgaged premises.

MORTGAGING OUT
Term applied to a mortgage that exceeds the current value of the property on which it is secured. This type of mortgage may be obtained on improvable property where the security is based on future value and future earnings that are expected to exceed construction costs.

MORTGAGOR
The borrower.

MULTI-FAMILY DWELLING
A property in which more than one suite is rentable.

MULTIPLE LISTING SERVICE (MLS)
Trademark owned by the Canadian Real Estate Association. Used in conjunction with a real estate database service operated by local real estate boards under which properties may be listed, purchased and sold.

N

NATIONAL HOUSING ACT (NHA)
The *National Housing Act* (1954) provides for insuring loans made by approved lenders and for direct mortgage lending under a variety of programs by Canada Mortgage and Housing Corporation (CMHC) to improve housing conditions in Canada.

NATIONAL HOUSING ACT MORTGAGE
A first mortgage, originated by an approved lender, granted under the terms of, and insured under, the *National Housing Act* of 1954.

NEGATIVE CASH FLOW
Where operating costs exceed gross rental income or debts.

NET OPERATING INCOME (NOI)
The balance remaining after deduction of operating expenses from gross receipts and gross rental, but not including the deducting of debt service on mortgages. Free and clear return on property is calculated by the ratio of NOI to total investment, including mortgages and equity. This gives a direct means of comparing the return on different properties.

NET RATE OF INTEREST
The interest rate received by a mortgage lender net of the servicing fee deducted by a loan correspondent.

NET WORTH
A person's total financial worth, determined by subtracting total liabilities from total assets.

NOMINAL INTEREST RATE
Often referred to as "effective rate." The interest rate stated on the face of a loan document. However, if the loan amount is discounted or sold at premium, the effective rate of interest will either be higher or lower.

NON-RECOURSE LOAN
A loan clause that waives personal liability of the borrower on the loan.

NOTICE DOR
Notice filed in court by mortgagor under foreclosure proceedings that he desires an opportunity to redeem and make good on past due balances.

O

OAC
On approved credit.

OBLATORY ADVANCE
An advance made according to terms of a pre-existing construction loan agreement or mortgage.

OFFER TO PURCHASE
A written proposal to purchase real estate that becomes binding upon acceptance of the vendor.

OPEN OR CLOSED
The restriction or denial of repayment rights until the maturity of the mortgage is a "closed" mortgage. If specified on the document as "open," then the mortgagor can pay extra payments of principal sums at any time or at specified times, with or without repayment penalty.

OPEN-END MORTGAGE
A mortgage under which the lender has the option of advancing more funds where, for example, the value of the property is anticipated to increase.

OPERATING EXPENSES
Generally speaking, all expenses, occurring periodically, which are necessary to produce net income before depreciation. Under some conditions these expenses are placed in two categories, namely, operating expenses and fixed charges.

OPTION
A right given by the owner of a property to another (for valuable consideration) to buy a certain property within a limited time at an agreed price; an option holder who does not buy at or within the specified period loses the deposit and the agreement is cancelled.

OWNER
The lawful possessor of the title to real property.

P

PACKAGE LOAN
A combination of two types of loans, e.g., a construction loan and permanent financing. The borrower benefits by having to negotiate with a single lender and having to pay a single set of closing costs.

PARTIAL DISCHARGE
A discharge of a definite portion of the mortgage lands, usually given after the mortgagor has prepaid a specific portion of the mortgage debt.

PARTICIPATION LOAN
An agreement whereby two or more lenders share in advancing a portion of a loan made by the originating or "lead" bank. Terms of the agreement set out a method of apportionment and interest rates. The lead lender generally services the loan, for which it receives a fee.

PERCENT PAID OFF
The percent of principal that is paid off at a given time under an amortization schedule, i.e., equity build-up.

PERCENTAGE RENTAL AGAINST MINIMUM
A rental paid under a percentage lease whereby rent paid by a tenant varies according to the volume of business, e.g., a percentage of gross receipts, sales or revenue is paid to the extent that it exceeds a minimum rental.

PERCENTAGE RENT PLUS MINIMUM
A percentage rental that must be paid in addition to the minimum; minimum rent is not credited against percentage rent payable.

PERMANENT FINANCING
A long-term mortgage, usually intended to finance both land and improvements after

completion of construction; it is used to pay off a construction loan.

PERSONAL LIABILITY
A person is liable on a debt to the full extent of his or her entire assets, as opposed to limited liability where a maximum or ceiling is fixed on the amount of assets that can be drawn upon to satisfy a debt. Joint and several liability fixes the liability of each individual borrower for the total debt; joint liability binds all the borrowers together in one action; and several liability fixes the liability of each borrower to the extent of his or her share of the debt.

PERSONAL PROPERTY
All property except land and the improvements thereon.

POINTS
Discount charges imposed by lenders to raise the yield of their loan. One point equals 1 percent.

POLARIS
The Province of Ontario Land Registration Improvement System's new simplified method of registration of transfer, charge, discharge, etc.

PORTABILITY
A mortgage option that enables borrowers to take their mortgage with them to another property without penalty. A transfer fee may apply.

POSTPONEMENT CLAUSE
A junior mortgage may contain a postponement clause, by which the mortgagee permits the borrower to renew or replace an existing first mortgage that falls due prior to the maturity date of the junior mortgage.

POWER OF SALE
The right of a mortgagee to force the sale of the property without judicial proceedings should default occur.

PREPAYMENT CLAUSE
A clause inserted in a mortgage that gives the mortgagor the privilege of paying off all or part of the mortgage debt in advance of the maturity date.

PREPAYMENT PENALTY
The sum of money (the amount of extra interest as set out in the mortgage document) a

mortgagee may require from a mortgagor to exercise the option in a mortgage to prepay any outstanding principal.

PRE-QUALIFICATION
An interview with a client (usually) prior to the writing of an offer to purchase real estate in order to determine the applicant's qualifications for a mortgage.

PRIME RATE
The rate charged by banks to their most credit-worthy borrowers. Sometimes referred to as the rate of interest paid on government bonds.

PRINCIPAL
The amount actually borrowed or still owing on a mortgage. Interest is paid on the principal amount.

PRIOR CHARGE
An encumbrance ranking in priority to the mortgage in question.

PRIOR ENCUMBRANCE
A claim on the property with priority ranking to the mortgage in question.

PRO FORMA STATEMENT
A financial statement of the gross income, operating costs, net operating costs and net operating income for a specified financial period, e.g., one year, using specified assumptions.

PROGRESS ADVANCES
Loan advances made on a property under construction whereby the lender makes advances on the basis of the retention at all times of an amount of the loan that in his/her opinion will be sufficient to complete the building, should the borrower fail to complete it.

PROJECTED INCOME
Estimated income from a property.

PROMISSORY NOTE
A written document acknowledging a debt and promising payment.

PROPERTY
Refers to the rights that an individual enjoys by virtue of his/her ownership.

PURCHASE-MONEY MORTGAGE
(Vendor take back)
A mortgage loan taken back by the vendor of a property in lieu of purchase money in order to help provide financing to the purchaser.

Q

QUALIFYING
The process of qualifying the borrower and/or lender to ensure they respectively have the financial ability and inclination to undertake the mortgage.

QUANTUM MERUIT
The amount that should be paid as merited by the service performed.

QUIT CLAIM DEED
A general release of all claims or rights to a parcel of land.

R

REAL ESTATE
Land, buildings and other fixed improvements, including items that are not moveable.

REAL ESTATE BOARD
Non-profit organization representing local real estate brokers/agents/salespeople. Provides services to its members and maintains and operates an MLS system in the community.

REALTOR
A real estate broker holding active membership in a local real estate board.

REDEMPTION
The buying back of a mortgage estate by payment of the sum due on the mortgage.

REDEMPTION PERIOD
A period of time allowed by law during which a mortgagor may redeem his or her property by paying off the entire debt in arrears.

REFINANCE
To pay off (discharge) a mortgage and other registered encumbrances by arranging a new mortgage.

REGISTRATION AND DISCHARGE DATES
Dates of registration by number in the local Registry Office and/or Land Titles Office, which are then given to the mortgagee. When the loan has been paid in full at or after maturity date, the mortgagee executes the "discharge" or cessation of charge and registers same to liquidate the mortgage and allow the mortgagor to redeem the mortgage.

RELEASE OF COVENANT
A release given to the mortgagor of a property that has been sold to a new purchaser, who is acceptable to the mortgagee. This release is usually given after the new mortgagor has signed an assumption agreement.

RENEWAL AGREEMENT
An agreement whereby the lender may agree to extend the loan, but possibly on revised terms as to principal repayments and interest rate.

RENT CONTRACT
Rental received by the real estate owner under any lease contract.

RENTAL HOLDBACK
STANDBY LOAN
A holdback is an amount withheld from the borrower under permanent financing until a certain occupancy rate is achieved. As this deprives the construction lender of full takeout protection, the developer may obtain a standby loan commitment to supplement the holdback.

RENTAL REQUIREMENTS
This is the "ceiling" portion of a permanent loan commitment that is advanced upon reaching a minimum rental or occupancy rate.

RENTAL VALUE
The monetary amount reasonably expectable for the right to the agreed use of real estate. It may be expressed as an amount per month or other period of time, or per room, per frontal foot or other unit of property.

RENT ECONOMIC
The income that real estate can command in the open market at any given time for its highest and best use.

REPRODUCTION COST
The cost of reproducing a new replica property on the basis of current prices with the same or very similar materials.

RESTRICTION
A limitation placed upon the use of property contained in the deed or other written instrument in the chain of title.

RESTS
The periodic balancing of an account made for the purpose of converting interest into principal and charging the party liable thereon with compound interest.

RETURN ON INVESTMENT (ROI)
(a) Free and clear return is calculated as the percentage of net operating income to total investment in the property; (b) Cash flow return is the ratio of cash flow to equity investment (also known as return on equity and cash-on-cash return); (c) Total return is cash flow, including loan amortization as a percentage of the total invested.

REVERSION
The right to repossess and resume the full and sole use and proprietorship of real property that temporarily has been alienated by lease, easement or otherwise. According to the terms of the controlling instrument, the reversionary right becomes effective at a stated time or under certain conditions, such as the termination of a leasehold, abandonment of a right-of-way or at the end of the economic life of the improvements. It is the present or discounted value of something to be collected at some future date.

RIGHT
The interest one has in a piece of property, i.e., a claim or title enforceable by law.

RIGHT OF SURVIVORSHIP
The distinguishing feature of joint tenancies that provides that, where land is held in undivided portions by co-owners, upon the death of any joint owner, his/her interest in the land will pass to the surviving co-owner, rather than to his/her estate.

RIGHT OF WAY
The right to pass over another's land, more or less frequently, according to the nature of an easement.

RIPARIAN RIGHTS
The rights of owners of land on the banks of watercourses to take advantageous use of the water on, under or adjacent to their land,

including the right to acquire wharf slips and fish from them.

RUNNING WITH THE LAND
A covenant is said to run with the land when it extends beyond the original parties to the agreement and binds all subsequent owners to either liability to perform it or the right to take advantage of it.

S

SALE AND LEASEBACK
A method of financing where a property is sold to a purchaser who simultaneously enters into a long-term lease of the property with the vendor. The vendor (now lessee) remains in possession for the specified term of the lease and agrees to pay the rental to this purchaser (now lesser) as well as all operation expenses. This enables the user to free his or her cash investment in the real property for some other use.

SALES HOLDBACK
A percentage of the principal amount of the mortgage held back by the mortgagee until the property in question has been sold to a party satisfactory to the mortgagee.

SANDWICH LEASE
A lease in which the "sandwich party" is the lessee of one party and the lesser to another. Usually, the owner of the sandwich lease is neither the fee owner nor the user of the property.

SEALED AND DELIVERED
A term indicating that a conveyor has received adequate consideration as evidenced by his/her voluntary delivery. The word "sealed" adds more strength, since under old conveyance law an official seal was used as a substitute for consideration.

SECOND MORTGAGE
A mortgage loan granted (and registered) when there is already a first mortgage registered against the property, usually with shorter terms and a higher interest rate than the first mortgage.

SECURED CREDITOR
A creditor who has one or more forms of security that gives a prior claim on the security in case of default.

SELLER FINANCING
When an owner of a property provides the purchaser with a mortgage (or other financing) so that the buyer does not have to obtain any or all of the financing from another source.

SELLER'S AGENT
Represents the seller as a listing agent under the listing agreement with the seller, or by co-operating as a sub-agent, typically through the MLS system.

SERVIENT TENEMENT
An estate or land over which an easement or some other service exists in favour of the dominant tenement.

SETBACK
The distance from the curb or other established line within which no buildings may be erected.

SHORT-FORM MORTGAGE
A mortgage document that follows the exact language of the long form prescribed by law but is abbreviated, using shortened terminology. It has the identical legal effect of a long-form mortgage.

SINGLE-FAMILY DWELLING
A residential property designed for occupancy by one family and situated on land zoned specifically for that purpose.

SPECIFIC PERFORMANCE
A remedy in a court of equity compelling a defendant to carry out the terms of an agreement or contract. It is available only where the remedy of damages cannot afford adequate relief to the plaintiff.

SPECULATIVE BUILDER OR DEVELOPER
One who builds without having a commitment to buy or lease from a purchaser or tenant.

STANDBY COMMITMENT
A commitment from a lender to make a loan in a specified period of time, on specified terms, with the understanding that the borrower will not likely draw down the funds.

STATEMENT OF ADJUSTMENTS
A balance statement prepared by lawyers setting out the details of a mortgage transaction.

It indicates credits to the vendor, such as the purchase price and any prepaid taxes, and credits to the buyer, such as the deposit and the balance due on closing.

STATUS CERTIFICATE
(also called an estoppel certificate)
A written statement or certificate that states certain facts upon which the receiver of the statement or a third party may rely, e.g., a lender's estoppel statement as to a purchaser or property. The lender cannot later deny the truth of these statements because a third party has relied and acted upon them.

STATUTE
A law established by an act of the legislature.

STATUTE OF FRAUDS
A law that provides that certain contracts must be in writing in order to be enforceable by law. It includes real estate contracts.

STATUTE OF LIMITATIONS
That period of time specified by statute within which an action at law must be brought or else be forfeited.

STEP-DOWN LEASE
A lease providing for decreases in rental payment at specified dates.

STEP-UP LEASE
A lease providing for increases in rental payment at specified dates.

SUBORDINATION CLAUSE
A mortgage clause that gives priority to a mortgage taken out at a later date.

SURVEY
A document that illustrates a property's boundaries and measurements, the position of major structures on that property and any registered or viable easements.

SURVIVORSHIP
The right of a person to secure ownership by reason of his/her outliving someone with whom he/she shared undivided interest in the land.

T

TAKEOUT MORTGAGE LOAN

A long-term mortgage loan that is advanced to a borrower on completion of construction or in compliance with any other conditions in the loan commitment. The funds are normally used to pay off or take out the construction lender.

TAX LIEN

A lien imposed by a taxing authority on real estate for failure to pay taxes within the time required by law.

TENANCY AT WILL

A licence to use or occupy lands and buildings at the will of the owner.

TENANCY IN COMMON

Ownership of and by two or more persons. Unlike joint tenancy, the interest of the deceased does not pass to the survivor but is treated as an asset of the deceased's estate.

TENURE

A system of land holdings for a temporary time period.

TERM (OF LOAN)

The length of time that a mortgage agreement covers. Payments made may not repay the outstanding principal by the end of the term because of a longer amortization period. Also indicates when the principal balance becomes due and payable to the lender.

TIME IS OF THE ESSENCE

Requires punctual performance of a contract on closing date and is indicated by so stating, as in an Agreement of Purchase and Sale.

TITLE

The means of evidence by which the owner of land has lawful ownership thereof. A freehold title gives the holder full and exclusive ownership of land and buildings for an indefinite period of time; in condominium ownership, land and common elements of buildings are owned collectively by all unit owners, while the residential units belong exclusively to the individual owners; a leasehold title gives the holder a right to use and occupy land and buildings for a defined period of time.

TITLE INSURANCE

A policy that insures the lender and purchaser against loss due to a flaw in the title of property held as collateral for a mortgage.

TITLE RESTRICTION

A restriction in a deed to limit or govern the use of the land.

TITLE SEARCH

An examination of the chain of title to real property as indicated in the public records in order to determine the ownership of the property and the existence of any encumbrances or defects.

TORRENS SYSTEM

Also known as the "Land Titles System." System of recording titles provided by provincial law. It is a system for the registration of land title, indicating the state of the title, including ownership and encumbrances without the necessity of an additional search of the public records.

TOTAL DEBT SERVICE (TDS)

The percentage of gross annual income required to cover payments associated with housing and all other debts and obligations.

TRANSFER

To convey from one person to another.

TRANSFER OF CHARGE

Assignment of a mortgage under the Land Titles System.

U

UMBRELLA MORTGAGE

Also referred to as a "wrap-around mortgage." A special arrangement whereby one document encompasses one or more already existing mortgages registered on the same property. The mortgagee is responsible for remission of payment(s) to lender(s), while the mortgagor makes one payment to the mortgagee.

UNDERWRITER (MORTGAGE)

A person employed by a mortgage lender or mortgage broker who approves or turns down loan applications based upon the quality of the real property, the credit-worthiness and ability of the applicant to pay, as well as guidelines of the lender with regard to the ratio of the mortgage loan to the value of the property.

V

VALID
Having force or binding force that is legally sufficient and authorized by law.

VALUABLE CONSIDERATION
The granting of some beneficial right, interest or profit for suffering of some detrimental forbearance, loss or default by one party in exchange for the performance of another.

VARIABLE INTEREST MORTGAGE
A loan where the interest rate may vary during the term of the mortgage. The variance is usually tied to some specific factor such as the prime bank rate or the guaranteed investment certificate rate for a designated lender.

VENDOR
A seller of real property.

VENDOR-TAKE-BACK MORTGAGE
A mortgage that a vendor of real property takes from the purchaser, usually as part payment of the purchase price for that property.

VOID
Of no legal effect; a nullity.

VOIDABLE
Where one party to a contract is entitled to rescind the contract at his or her option.

W

WAIVER
An international relinquishment of some right or interest; the renunciation, abandonment or surrender of some claim.

WITNESS
To subscribe one's name to a deed, will or other document for the purpose of attesting its authenticity and proving its execution by testifying, if required.

WRAP-AROUND MORTGAGE
Sometimes erroneously called a blanket mortgage. A new mortgage that is registered on title and that includes a prior existing mortgage. The new mortgagee undertakes the responsibility as mortgagor under the original mortgage.

Y – Z

YIELD
The return on an investment expressed as a percentage per annum of the amount invested.

ZONING
The public regulation of the character and intensity of the use of real estate through the employment of police power. This is accomplished by the establishment of districts in each of which uniform holding restrictions related to use, height, area, bulk and density of population are imposed upon the private property.

Note to Reader: These terms are intended as quick references only. Be sure to seek legal or accounting advice for all of your real estate transactions.

REAL ESTATE INVESTMENT NETWORK – REIN™

The Real Estate Investment Network (REIN) is a research and education company dedicated to providing real estate investors with unbiased research and strategies for the Canadian marketplace. Members of the REIN community meet monthly in select cities across the country. Some of its members live outside Canada and receive full CDs of the live events. REIN is now entering its 18th year of operation and has continued to provide research and support in all market conditions. Whether an investor is buying, selling or holding, REIN's research and strategies are a valuable tool to reducing risk and maximizing returns. REIN's research has assisted members in safely and securely purchasing over $3.1 billion of Canadian residential real estate. It is important to note that REIN does not sell property to their clients. REIN's members focus on long-term wealth as opposed to getting rich quick. This success comes from focusing on real-life economic fundamentals and putting the ACRE system into action. This system takes the hype out of the marketplace so you can focus on what works right in your backyard.

REIN is an exclusive paid-membership program, which is dedicated to educating its members about how, where and when to buy Canadian real estate. From networking with other active investors, to providing direct access to leading-edge experts, it is the most complete program of its kind anywhere in North America. You will never have to buy from, invest with or put money into any real estate deal with anyone in, or associated with, REIN.

REIN's single objective is to help you become an experienced, confident and wealthy real estate investor. There are no huge upfront seminar fees; REIN believes that money is best spent investing in real estate—not on seminars.

To receive a FREE 12-page package on the benefits of being a member of Canada's most successful real estate investment program, with over $3.1 billion purchased and over 18 years of market experience both up and down, call 1-888-824-7346 today or e-mail your mailing address and telephone number to Don R. Campbell's office at info@reincanada.com. You can also visit www.realestateinvestingincanada.com and click on the REIN button. We look forward to helping you achieve what members of REIN call, your own "Personal Belize."

WEB SITES FOR THE REAL ESTATE INVESTOR

Sophisticated real estate investors know information is power and when it comes to the tax and accounting implications of real estate investment, a lot of the information you need is embedded in federal and provincial legislation.

The REIN Web site, **www.realestateinvestingincanada.com**, is Canada's most trusted source of unbiased real estate investment news, research and information.

Here are a few of the government Web sites you need to bookmark—and learn to find your way around.

Canadian Revenue Agency
www.cra-arc.ca

Alberta
www.albertacanada.com/statpub/

British Columbia
www.fin.gov.bc.ca/pubs.html

Manitoba
www.gov.mb.ca/queensprinter

New Brunswick
www.snb.ca/e/6000/6300e.asp

Newfoundland
www.nf.ca/publicat/

North West Territories
www.gov.nt.ca/research/publication/index.html

Nova Scotia
www.gov.ns.ca/

Nunavut
www.gov.nu.ca/

Ontario
www.publications.serviceontario.ca/ecom

Prince Edward Island
www.gov.pe.ca/pt/taxandland/index.php3

Quebec
www.publicationsduquebec.gouv.qc.ca/accueil.fr.html

Saskatchewan
www.publications.gov.sk.ca/legislation.cfm

Yukon
www.gov.yk.ca/pubs/

AN OPEN LETTER TO THE READER

Dear Reader,

It is our hope that *81 Tips* has given you new ideas that you will put into action to make your real estate investments more profitable. And by purchasing this book, you have helped Habitat for Humanity build housing for those in need. We thank you.

We are pleased to announce forthcoming books written by veteran real estate investors that you may wish to add to your reference library, and to remind you of books that are available that have been written specifically for you, the Canadian real estate investor.

As always, we invite you to visit our web site for more information about REIN, our membership, and products and services we deliver to the investor community, and wish you every success in achieving your investment goals.

Sincerely,

Don R. Campbell
President, REIN

REAL ESTATE INVESTING IN CANADA

2.0

CREATING WEALTH WITH THE *ACRE* SYSTEM

Revised & Updated with FREE Property Analyzer Software that will help investors reduce risks and increase returns in any market conditions

Revised & Updated with FREE Property Analyzer Software that will help investors reduce risks and increase returns in any market conditions

Revised & Updated with FREE Property Analyzer Software that will help investors reduce risks and increase returns in any market conditions

REAL ESTATE INVESTING IN CANADA: CREATING WEALTH WITH THE ACRE SYSTEM 2.0

Don R. Campbell

Canada's #1 selling real estate guide.

In *Real Estate Investing in Canada 2.0*, investors will learn about the updates to the Authentic Canadian Real Estate (ACRE) system, a step-by-step system designed to show how to invest in real estate profitably. Cutting through the real estate hype with honest and proven advice, Don Campbell covers such topics as:

- How to spot an under- or over-priced market
- How to analyze any property
- How to tell if a town will boom or bust
- The 18 secrets of getting the deal you want
- The seven proven strategies that will get the bank to say "yes" to your deal
- New financial strategies and assessment tools.

The fundamentals of the real estate market have changed dramatically in the past few years as markets are beginning to cool off after a string of rapid increases. This new edition of *Real Estate Investing in Canada* will show readers how to get in, and just as importantly, how to get out of the market to protect their investments.

Don R. Campbell is a real estate investor, consultant and the President of Canada's Real Estate Investment Network (REIN). He is also the best-selling author of Real *Estate Investing in Canada* and *97 Tips for Canadian Real Estate Investors.*

Available now!

97 TIPS FOR CANADIAN REAL ESTATE INVESTORS

2.0

DON R. CAMPBEL

PETER KINCH | BARRY MCGUIRE | RUSSELL WESTCO...

97 Tips for Canadian Real Estate Investors 2.0

Don R. Campbell, Peter Kinch, Barry McGuire, and Russell Westcott

Whether you are a beginning investor or own a portfolio of residential units, *97 Tips for Canadian Real Estate Investors 2.0* provides you with insights, strategies and success stories to help you build wealth faster and save time and money.

You'll discover the challenges and pitfalls the authors have experienced—and learn how to avoid them. They will outline success strategies based on the proven Authentic Canadian Real Estate System that works in markets all across Canada, time and time again. From understanding the principles and economics of investing, to sourcing properties and financing, closing deals and becoming a landlord, *97 Tips* is chockfull of great ideas for investors who want to achieve beyond their dreams.

Don R. Campbell is a real estate investor, consultant and the President of Canada's Real Estate Investment Network ™ (REIN). He is also the best-selling author of *Real Estate Investing in Canada 2.0* and *Secrets of the Canadian Real Estate Cycle*.

Peter Kinch is the founder of The Peter Kinch Mortgage Team and the PK-Approved Dominion Lending Centres network of brokers across Canada. He is well-known in the media, a regular contributor to the *Western Investor* and other periodicals.

Barry McGuire is an experienced real estate lawyer who enjoys a diversified real estate investment portfolio, and has been investing for more than 30 years.

Russell Westcott is a veteran real estate investor, researcher and educator and is a Vice President of the Real Estate Investment Network.

Available now!

DON R. CAMPBELL | KIERAN TRASS | GREG HE

SECRETS OF THE
CANADIAN
REAL
ESTATE
CYCLE

AN INVESTOR'S GUIDE

with CHRISTINE RUPTASH

Secrets of the Canadian Real Estate Cycle: An Investor's Guide

Don R. Campbell, Kieran Trass, Greg Head, Christine Ruptash

Is that it? Is the Canadian real estate boom finally ending? After a long-running boom in the real estate market, many involved in the realm of Canadian real estate expect to see a period of slower growth or declining values, but this doesn't mean that investors necessarily need to cool their heels, sell everything or go on a buying spree. The reality is that all real estate markets around the world operate on a cycle, from Boom to Slump, Slump to Recovery, and from Recovery back Boom. The key for investors is to be able to identify exactly where in the real estate cycle their target area is and how to take advantage of this knowledge, as there is money to be made in all of the phases.

The real estate cycle has been in existence for a long time yet many investors have little understanding of how it materially impacts real estate over time. An entire real estate cycle can typically take a decade or more to complete, which can explain why many home buyers and investors fail to recognize that there is a cycle to it all. But once you understand the cycle and what drives it, you become empowered to use your knowledge of the cycle to your advantage. During the specific phases of the real estate cycle there are "cyclically sensible" actions that wise investors take, and other actions they avoid, because they are not "cyclically sensible." Another key element of the cycle is the availability of financing, which is directly related to the phases of the cycle.

Written by a team of investment professionals that includes Don R Campbell, Canada's top-selling real estate author; Keiran Trass, a leading international expert on real estate cycles; Greg Head, a Canadian investment specialist; and writer and real estate enterpreneur Christine Ruptash, you'll learn about the key factors that drive cycles, and those that have lesser impact, to enable you to assess your local market and decide which investment tactics will produce the best results for you.

Complete with charts, checklists, and real-life stories, Secrets of the Canadian Real Estate Cycle is an indispensable guide that will teach you how to become a strategic investor and profit in every market.

SOUTH
OF 49

**THE CANADIAN GUIDE
TO BUYING RESIDENTIAL
REAL ESTATE IN
THE UNITED STATES**

PHILIP McKERNAN
DAN SAMPSON | MIKE CUNNING

SOUTH OF 49

THE CANADIAN GUIDE TO BUYING RESIDENTIAL REAL ESTATE IN THE UNITED STATES

Philip McKernan, Dan Sampson, Mike Cunning

Avoid the pitfalls and capitalize on the buyer's market in prime American cities.

The dramatic real estate collapse in the United States has presented investors with a once-in-a-lifetime opportunity to scoop up properties at rock-bottom prices. As shrewd as it may seem, buying real estate in the U.S. can pose all sorts of unexpected challenges and pitfalls for Canadian purchasers. Based on the authors' real life experiences and proprietary research, *South of 49* covers such topics as:

• The differences between Canadian and U.S. real estate laws
• Tax regulations affecting foreign buyers
• Financing strategies
• How to target locations with a potential for cash flow and equity growth
• Buying foreclosed properties.

Filled with tested and practical advice, *South of 49* is the perfect entry-level primer for any Canadian investor looking to profit from the depressed real estate market in the United States.

Philip McKernan is founder and president of the real estate investment company Maple Leaf Property. His investment portfolio includes properties in Ireland, the United Kingdom, France, Finland, South Africa and North America. For more information about Philip, real estate mentoring and events, see www.southof49.com.

Dan Sampson (Vancouver, BC) and Mike Cunning (Vancouver, BC) bring a wealth of real estate knowledge to *South of 49*. Their combined expertise includes urban planning, building and renovation, and property conversion and management.

THE REAL ESTATE SOLUTION FOR YOUR RRSP

Build Wealth Quickly Using a Secret Strategy of The Very Rich

GREG HABSTRITT

Founder, Masterwealth Training Inc.

THE REAL ESTATE SOLUTION FOR YOUR RRSP

BUILD WEALTH QUICKLY USING A SECRET STRATEGY OF THE VERY RICH

Greg Habstritt

One RRSP plan your bank will **not** tell you about.

Millions of Canadians faithfully contribute to their RRSPs on the advice of so-called experts only to find out that not only do they not have enough to retire, but that the institutions that sold them these products in the first place produce record profits year after year. The good news is that it is indeed possible to achieve double-digit returns and build wealth much quicker than what banks have on offer. In *Real Estate Investing and Your RRSP*, Greg Habstritt, a seasoned real estate investor, spells out a proven strategy that shows how ordinary Canadians can shelter their real estate investments in their RRSP. Covered topics include:

- Why the financial industry does not serve the individual investor
- Why Canadians do not hear about higher return, lower risk strategies
- The secrets of the most powerful RRSP strategy – private mortgages
- Private syndications and public real estate investment trusts

Full of applicable tips and clear, actionable advice, *Real Estate Investing and Your RRSP* will appeal to all Canadian investors fed up with mediocre returns who want to get back on the road to building wealth and financial freedom.

Greg Habstritt is an entrepreneur, real estate investor, speaker, and financial counselor.

Available April 2010

THE CANADIAN
REAL ESTATE
ACTION
PLAN

Proven Investment
Strategies to **Kick-Start**
and **Build** Your Portfolio

Peter Kinch

Foreword by Don R. Campbell

THE CANADIAN REAL ESTATE ACTION PLAN
PROVEN INVESTMENT STRATEGIES TO KICK START AND BUILD YOUR PORTFOLIO

Peter Kinch

A simple plan for all real estate investors.

More and more Canadians are turning to real estate as their primary investment vehicle. Financing these real estate acquisitions is a crucial component that many investors do not understand well enough, often resulting in an incomplete financial plan and unnecessary risk-taking. *The Canadian Real Estate Action Plan* aims to educate investors on how to properly finance their portfolios and implement a specific plan best suited to their situation. The four key themes covered in the book include:

- Understanding the seven financial 'sandbox rules' imposed by lenders
- Developing investment objectives and planning for success
- Financing strategies to implement the plan
- Specific tools and products for the experienced investor

Filled with tips and advice on everything from developing a portfolio strategy to tax minimization, leveraging home equity, debt-service ratios and joint venture partnerships, *The Canadian Real Estate Action Plan* is a must-read guide for all Canadian real estate investors.

Peter Kinch is the founder of The Peter Kinch Mortgage Team and the PK-Approved Dominion Lending Centres network of brokers across Canada. He is well-known in the media, a regular contributor to the *Western Investor* and other periodicals and co-author of the #1 bestseller *97 Tips for Canadian Real Estate Investors*.

Available July 2010

REAL ESTATE
JOINT VENTURES
FOR CANADIAN
INVESTORS

A PROVEN AND POWERFUL STEP-BY-STEP SYSTEM

DON R. CAMPBELL & RUSSELL WESTCOTT

REAL ESTATE JOIN VENTURES FOR CANADIAN INVESTORS

A PROVEN AND POWERFUL STEP-BY-STEP SYSTEM

Don R. Campbell & Russell Westcott

Learn the power of partnership in real estate investing.

Don Campbell, Canada's #1 real estate investing guru, has shown that just about anyone can start investing in real estate profitably if they follow his rules. In his latest book, Campbell will show readers that the key to real wealth and success are joint ventures with like-minded investors. *Real Estate Joint Ventures for Canadian Investors* will guide readers through the secrets and strategies of how joint ventures work, including:

- Creating a win-win relationship with your partners
- Screening and attracting the right partners—and capital
- Joint venture legal structures and agreements
- 19 landmines to avoid in joint venture partnerships

Filled with helpful insights and Canadian-specific tips, there's no other book like this on the market.

Don R. Campbell is a real estate investor, consultant and the President of Canada's Real Estate Investment Network (REIN). He is also the best-selling author of Real *Estate Investing in Canada* and *97 Tips for Canadian Real Estate Investors*.

Russell Westcott is Vice President at REIN and co-author of *97 Tips for Canadian Real Estate Investors*.

Available October 2010

ACKNOWLEDGEMENTS

Real estate is a team sport, and so is creating a book that has depth, facts and details. The team who created this book are second to none with their dedication to accuracy and making a difference in as many people's lives as possible. And for this I thank Navaz Murji and George Dube for all of their hard work in transferring the complex subject of Canadian tax law into a resource that Canadians at all levels can use.

I also appreciate the "special guest" contributions to Sophisticated Investor Tips made by my wife, Connie, whose experience on the real estate investment accounting front pre-dates the launch of our own real estate investment portfolio.

All of us also owe a big debt of gratitude to Joy Gregory who helped to make this book a cohesive reference guide by combining all of our ideas and research into one voice. Joy, you are the absolute best at what you do in Canada.

And finally, without the leadership and championing of this book by our editor Don Loney, and the support of the Wiley team, this book would never have even been started.

Thank you to all who are taking control of their financial future and to all who purchase this book. As 100% of all the author royalties are being donated directly to Habitat for Humanity in Canada, you are making a difference, too.

ABOUT THE AUTHORS

Don R. Campbell is the author of the Canadian bestseller *Real Estate Investing in Canada 2.0*, a book that all real estate investors should have as an action tool and reference. A staunch advocate of the Authentic Canadian Real Estate System (ACRES), Don is president of the Real Estate Investment Network (REIN). REIN membership exceeds 3,000 successful Canadian investors whose investment in Canadian residential real estate tops $3.4 billion.

At real estate seminars and live workshops held across the country, Don shares his years of hands-on experience as he teaches strategies he has personally tested in the real world. Through REIN (www.reincanada.com), Don has helped investors achieve their dreams. Some of the most notable investor stories were the foundation of another of his books, *51 Success Stories from Canadian Real Estate Investors*. Along the way, charities such as Habitat for Humanity have also benefited from Don's enterprise.

He provides regular updates and insights on his blog at www. DonRCampbell.com and on Twitter at www.twitter.com/donrcampbell.

George E. Dube, Chartered Accountant, is a veteran real estate accountant and investor. George and his partner, Peter Cuttini, CA, CPA, focus on providing the knowledge and tools clients need to increase and preserve the value of their businesses. They deal with real estate accounting for clients across Canada and around the world, with a particular focus on Canadian and US investments.

George is a frequent guest speaker at various events, meetings, and workshops. There, he addresses a variety of tax and accounting topics with implications for real estate investors, with a particular focus on tax strategies. He talks about ways investors can improve communication with their accountants and better organize their financial affairs, and developed the accountant in-a-box™ program (www.accountantinabox.ca), to help investors do just that.

George established the predecessor to Dube & Cuttini Chartered Accountants LLP, in 1997 after several years with national accounting firms. He is a graduate of the University of Waterloo's Master of Accounting Program, where he completed a double specialization in Taxation and Public Accounting. He also completed the Canadian Institute of Chartered Accountants' two-year In-Depth Taxation Course.

George has written and contributed to articles in various national and regional publications. He has also co-authored *Legal, Tax & Accounting Strategies for the Canadian Real Estate Investor* (Cohen and Dube: Wiley 2010).

Navaz Murji is a Certified General Accountant (CGA). In 1992, he moved his nine-year-old accounting practice to Burnaby, B.C., from Edmonton, where he had already started investing in real estate. Today's practice, Murji & Associates (www.realaccountant.com), maintains a strong emphasis on owner-operated enterprises, with 48% of the client base comprised of real estate investors.

A strong believer in helping clients use internet-linked technology to manage their businesses, Navaz's expanding client base is located across Canada, but primarily focused on Alberta, B.C. and Ontario.

In addition to his successful accounting practice, Navaz holds a real estate investment portfolio that gives him real-world experience with real estate investing. His present portfolio includes several multi-family buildings developed with other investors. He also has extensive experience in the single-family home market, all of which makes a significant contribution to Navaz's ability to deliver real-world advice to his clientele.

INDEX OF FINANCIAL AND TAX TIPS

Tip #1: The truth about death and taxes.
Tip #2: Assemble your team.
Tip #3: Hire a qualified accountant
Tip #4: Get to know how the process of an accounting practice works.
Tip #5: There are questions you should *not ask* your accountant.
Tip #6: Learn to read financial statements.
Tip #7: Choose and use a record-keeping system.
Tip #8: All record-keeping programs are not created equal.
Tip #9: Know when to transition from DIY to bookkeeper and accountant.
Tip #10: Keep it simple. Keep it up to date!
Tip #11: Collect information, not stories.
Tip #12: Forget fairness. It's about the rules.
Tip #13: Never think you're special!
Tip #14: Review legal agreements for tax considerations.
Tip #15: Your home is your castle.
Tip #16: Once you decide who owns the property, you can't change it.
Tip #17: Incorporating my business makes sense when . . .
Tip #18: Pick the right bank account.
Tip #19: Get a separate bank account for your investment business.
Tip #20: Identify every deposit.
Tip #21: Manage your bank accounts with care.
Tip #22: Save the statements of adjustment and trust ledger statements
   for your accountant.
Tip #23: Keep your records clean.
Tip #24: Record loan principal at the time of financing.
Tip #25: Embrace technology that reduces record-keeping errors.
Tip #26: Keep permanent files.
Tip #27: Colour-code your filing system.
Tip #28: Protect yourself from fraud.
Tip #29: Pull all of these record-keeping tips together.
Tip #30: Go one step further and create a virtual office.
Tip #31: Receipts matter.

Tip #32: Expenses are real, not created.
Tip #33: Know how to define your expenses.
Tip #34: Remember to claim your indirect expenses.
Tip #35: Repairs and improvements are not the same thing with respect to a rental property.
Tip #36: Purchase your car personally.
Tip #37: You can deduct financing costs.
Tip #38: A loan can be interest deductible.
Tip #39: Documentation is key to deducting interest.
Tip #40: Closing documents include items with unique tax consequences.
Tip #41: Segregate principal and interest for mortgage payments.
Tip #42: Know what to do if you've missed a tax deduction or tax credit.
Tip #43: File and pay your taxes on time.
Tip #44: Know your tax deadlines.
Tip #45: Get your employee status definitions straight.
Tip #46: Understand the concept of marginal taxes.
Tip #47: Put your marginal tax rate to work.
Tip #48: Know the difference between a tax credit and a tax deduction.
Tip #49: Divide taxable income with income splitting.
Tip #50: Pay family members.
Tip #51: File T4s and T5s on time.
Tip #52: Formal reporting is especially important when dealing with family members.
Tip #53: Capital gain and income are *not* the same thing.
Tip #54: When it comes to capital gains, *intention* matters.
Tip #55: Look for ways to *prove* your primary intention.
Tip #56: The CRA will "look behind the curtain" for a backup plan!
Tip #57: Get to know the concept of capital cost allowance.
Tip #58: Make capital cost allowance work for you.
Tip #59: You *will be* audited.
Tip #60: Avoid unnecessary conflict with the auditor.
Tip #61: Reconsider self-representation.
Tip #62: Rule breakers invite scrutiny.
Tip #63: Statutes of limitations on audits.
Tip #64: Monitor your capital dividend account.
Tip #65: There may be tax implications to refinancing a property.
Tip #66: Use RDTOH to cut corporate taxes.